PLUS THE AMAZING KATZ KOLLECTION OF
JOKES AND STORIES AND FAMILY ANECDOTES

Papa, Play for Me

THE HILARIOUS, HEARTWARMING AUTOBIOGRAPHY

OF COMEDIAN AND BANDLEADER MICKEY KATZ

by
Mickey Katz

AS TOLD TO

Hannibal Coons

INTRODUCTION BY

Joel Grey

SIMON AND SCHUSTER   NEW YORK

DESIGNED BY EVE METZ
MANUFACTURED IN THE UNITED STATES OF AMERICA

1 2 3 4 5 6 7 8 9 10
LIBRARY OF CONGRESS CATALOGING IN PUBLICATION DATA
KATZ, MYRON.
PAPA, PLAY FOR ME.

1. KATZ, MYRON. 2. ENTERTAINERS—UNITED STATES—
BIOGRAPHY. I.COONS, HANNIBAL. II.TITLE.
PN2287.K27A36   790.2′092′4 [B]   77-9951
ISBN 0-671-22543-X

I dedicate this book to Grace, my loving wife of forty-seven years,
to my fine sons, Joel and Ron,
and their wives, Jo and Maddie,
and to my grandchildren, Randy, Jennifer, Todd, and Jimmy,
who have brought so much joy and love into my life.

Contents

Introduction

"You have to know where you've been in order to know where you're going." So says Stony McBride, the hero of John Guare's play *"Marco Polo Sings a Solo,"* to his mother, in an effort to fight off his collapsing world and to find some elusive missing pieces in the jigsaw puzzle of his life.

The production was at Joe Papp's Shakespeare Festival Theater in New York City, and I was in the midst of playing Stony when the manuscript for *Papa, Play for Me* arrived. I read it with enthusiasm and the expectancy that perhaps some secret puzzle pieces might be hidden in my father's book. And, in fact, they were. Pages, paragraphs, sentences, and words were pregnant, not with revelations of momentous events or insights, but rather with simple, intimate and personal reminders that clearly connected the present to the past for me.

It had never occurred to me why, every winter, I was a good deal more nervous than others about walking on New York's icy streets. In the early part of my father's book, I learned for the first time the circumstances of my paternal great-grandfather's death. And a tiny puzzle piece fell into place. He died of injuries sustained after a bad fall on the icy streets of Cleveland. The memory of that terrible event, I now know, must have been passed on to me in some subliminal way.

I had forgotten, or perhaps had never known, about the home remedy that Mother and Dad improvised to cure me of a bad bout with bronchial pneumonia that kept me out of school for nearly three months when I was fourteen. I laughed out loud at the naive but well-intentioned example of do-it-yourself medicine. I've always thought that deep down my father secretly yearned to be Dr. Mickey Katz, and had his fantasy come true, audiences might never have known the insane invention of "Duvid Crockett."

I'm remembering a time a number of years ago when my father was quite ill . . . and the tone in my brother's voice as he said it would be a good idea if I were to fly to Los Angeles as soon as possible. My wife and I were on the next plane, and I found myself filled with the strange and reflective melancholy that seems so often to accompany events of impending life-altering importance—births, deaths, long-term commitments.

We were standing at his hospital bed and when he realized we were there, he said to me, "I forgot to pick you up." He was weeping. "I'm sorry." I was confused until I realized that he was delirious and reliving a painful past experience. It seems I was six or seven years old. He was to pick me up at school, as always, but on this particular day his watch might have been incorrect, or he miscalculated the time—it makes no difference—the point is that I waited and waited at school and then walked home by myself. Naturally, I was confused and perhaps a bit frightened, but hardly scarred or traumatized; yet he took his responsibility so seriously, he cared so much, that even then, twenty-five years later, it remained in his thoughts.

My father and I have had the usual classic father-son struggles over the years, perhaps a bit more intense because of the added competitiveness of "following in Father's footsteps." Despite this, I always had the unalterable and unquestioned sense that my father was a man who cared enormously and consistently about us, about his parents, about his brother and sisters, about his friends, about others.

Just as strong in him was his commitment to his work. Even as a small boy, I felt his belief that an audience is always entitled to the very best an artist can give. In the early days, on those exhausting and underpaid one-niters, he would play as long as there was an audience that wanted him to. It would always be a treat when he would come home from work at four in the morning and wake me to share a bowl of raspberry Jello with sweet cream (he never had a good stomach).

I remember as a child going places with him—to the backstages of wherever he was working, to the music store to buy reeds for his clarinet, to the bakery, to my Uncle Al's drugstore . . . his usual rounds. He would always be welcomed by the people in those places with affection and respect, and he would always leave them certainly smiling, but more likely laughing.

As I grew older and had my own life working and traveling, no matter where I was, I would always be asked by his fans, "How's Dad?" "What's Mickey doing?" "We love your Daddy!" "Say 'hello' to Mick." "Sing 'Duvid Crockett.' " They spoke of him as if he were a close friend, and that good feeling toward him spilled over to me, and it still does.

Our beginnings have a power over each of us. "Grandma, tell us what it was like in Russia." "Grandma, tell us about the boat trip to America." "Dad, tell about the day I was born." And now, our children love poring over their baby pictures and asking us to tell them the familiar stories about "when they were little."

My father's book has naturally evoked all that for me—familiar things, stories, and yes, some puzzle pieces—but what affects me most is the book's expression of his life as a whole. The act of setting it all down is a powerful reminder to me of the depth and consistency of his caring and an accurate picture of Mickey Katz—musician, comedian, father, man.

JOEL GREY

1 · And Now—Heeerrrrrrre's Mickey!

ON A RECENT *Johnny Carson Show*, Johnny asked my son Joel Grey, "How come your name is Grey, and your father's name is Katz?"

Joel answered, "My father changed his name."

In the spring of 1967 there occurred an important happening in the Katz family. Joel and I were starring simultaneously on Broadway, in completely different musical revues. As far as I know, this had never before happened to a father and son in the whole Broadway scene. Joel was the Tony Award-winning star of *Cabaret,* playing at the Broadhurst Theater, and I was featured in *Hello, Solly* at the Henry Miller.

I was a proud papa, but my elation didn't last long. A few nights after *Hello, Solly* opened, I walked out on the stage at the Henry Miller Theater, sang my opening number, then walked to the microphone to greet the audience. Just then an elderly lady in the second row stood up and said, "Hey, Katz, I saw your boy Joel last night in *Cabaret.* He's better than you."

Taken by surprise, I said, "How can you say that? You haven't seen me do anything yet."

She said, "I've seen enough already."

This is a good example of the audience participation I have enjoyed in playing to Jewish audiences for the last thirty years. You can believe me that one of the most delightful descriptions of my audiences is that they don't consider the footlights any barrier between themselves and the actors. When they buy a ticket, it's like an invitation to a bar mitzvah or a wedding.

Mickele Rosenberg, the great Yiddish comedian, told a story about a young mother and her baby sitting in the front row of a theater he once played on New York's Lower East Side. In the middle of his performance the young lady took out a *zaftig* (ample) breast and tried to get her baby to nurse. But the baby stubbornly pushed her breast away. She pleaded with him aloud, *"Ess, ess!"* (Eat, eat!) But the baby still turned down the invitation. Finally, frustrated, she pointed toward the stage and told the baby, "Eat—or I'll give it to the actor."

One Sunday matinee at the Henry Miller there was a hilarious happening. Our Sunday matinee was always attended by an audience composed largely of senior citizens; their average age was around seventy-five, and many wore hearing aids. But we turned up the sound, and everybody usually had a good time.

But this particular Sunday, when we were just about to raise the curtain, the stage sound man came to my dressing room. He said, "Boy, are we in for it! One of the loudspeakers is dead—the sound is going to be too loud downstairs, and in the balcony they're not going to hear a thing." Oh, boy!

Well, the show must go on. I gave the cue to raise the curtain, the band played the overture, and I did my opening number; then I walked to the microphone and announced nice and clear, "Good afternoon, ladies and gentlemen. . . ."

At which moment a tiny ancient lady in the first row—she couldn't have been over four feet ten inches—stood up to her full height and gave out with a complaint. She said, "Who you yelling on!"

I said, "How are you, darling?"

She said, "Don't darlink me. Your microphone—it's too loud. It's breaking by me the ears." She pointed to a little man sitting alongside her, as ancient and tiny as she was; he looked like Noah without his Ark. She said, "This is my husband. He knows everything about microphones. Tell him what to do, Sam."

Sam got up and in a tiny voice said, "Stand a little foider back."

By this time I was open to suggestions. I moved back a few inches and started again: "Good afternoon, ladies and gentlemen. . . ."

Now a man in the balcony stood up and yelled, "Can't hear a woid!"

This went on during the whole show. People were jumping up all over the theater to voice personal complaints about our unfortunate situation. Believe me, that performance had a cast of a thousand.

But I love these audiences of senior citizens. Let me tell you about a special lady I love very much—my magnificent mother-in-law, Fanny.

Fanny, at eighty-nine, recently took a senior citizens' charter flight to Honolulu. Upon her return the family was naturally anxious to find out if she'd had a good time.

She said, "What good time? There were sixty of us; forty-four girls and only sixteen boys, who were running to the toilet every ten minutes. What a bunch of *alter kockers.*"

Grace asked, "Didn't you meet some younger people when you got to Honolulu?"

"Oh, when we got to the hotel, there were plenty young gentlemen. They were having a convention."

"What kind of convention, Mama?"

"It was the Kotex convention."

Grace said, "The Kotex convention—what were they showing in the exhibits?"

Her mother answered, "What else—cameras." It was the Kodak convention!

After Grace's dad passed away, her mother remarried at the age of seventy-four. A few weeks after the wedding Grace asked her mother if she and her new husband, Harry, were going on a honeymoon. She said, "Of course, we're going on a honeymoon. I've talked it over with Harry, and we're going to a movie."

My dear mother-in-law provides us with a lot of love and laughs. She and my wife, Grace, to whom I've been married for forty-seven years, and my sons, Joel and Ronnie, and the boys' wives and the four grandchildren—we all enjoy a wonderful relationship.

Except for the time when Joel and Ronnie decided we needed a dog.

Grace and I and Ronnie's family live in Los Angeles; Joel and his family live in New York. So we keep in touch by telephone. But when Joel comes to the Coast, he and Ronnie like to get together and shmooz a little about Mom and Dad.

When Joel came out to the Coast to perform the opening number of the Academy Awards show a few years ago, he knew it would require several weeks of rehearsal. So he took advantage of the opportunity for a family visit; instead of checking in at a hotel, he stayed with us at our home.

Since the house was in a secluded area, Joel and Ronnie decided that they should buy us a dog to protect us from the Beverly Hills bandits. Joel and Ronnie are both animal lovers; Joel has a dog and three cats in his apartment in New York, and Ronnie has two dogs in his house in Los Angeles. Not knowing how we would react to the suggestion, Joel broached the subject at dinner one night. He said, "Mom, Ronnie and I think you should have a dog."

Grace said, "Joel, I really don't think we need one, but if we were to have any kind of dog, I'd prefer a poodle."

Well, the next day about four in the afternoon Joel and Ronnie drove up, rang the doorbell, and when I opened the door, they dragged in this canine klutz—the biggest damned standard poodle you have ever seen. He looked not like a poodle, but like a white, untrimmed buffalo.

He took one look at me and growled. I had a premonition of impending disaster. The boys had brought some dog food for him, so I told them to put him and the dog food and a bowl of water in the kitchen. They fixed him up comfortably and left. They'd given Papa and Mama a swell dog.

They hadn't given us so much a swell dog as a *swollen* dog. Even if we could have gotten a leash on him, we couldn't have taken him anywhere, except to the zoo.

So for the next couple of days Joel rehearsed for the Academy Awards, Ronnie was busy at his office, Grace went to work every day at her art gallery—and I stayed home with the dog. Every time I got near the closed kitchen door he'd growl in a way that would have frightened King Kong. If that dog was man's best friend, I didn't need any enemies. When Grace got home, she'd open the kitchen door long enough to shove some food and more water at him, and we cleaned up the kitchen as best we could with a long-handled shovel. He was so big that he destroyed everything in the kitchen that he could chew up or knock over.

Meantime, Joel and Ronnie and the grandchildren were calling up delightedly to see how we liked our new dog. We were having a wonderful time. We couldn't get into the kitchen to cook, so we were sitting in the living room, eating Colonel Sanders chicken dinners. We tried to figure how we were going to get rid of the dog without hurting the family's feelings. We didn't want to hurt the grandchildren's feelings, and we didn't want to hurt the shmucky dog's feelings. But one of these days we were going to have to get back in our kitchen.

Joel, sensing that things weren't going too well, said, "Dad, what you need to do is take him for a walk." Joel is not easily daunted, and he came over one day between rehearsals, got a leash on the dog, and we took him—dragged him—out for a walk. On the way Joel kept trying to give me lessons in "Bringing Up Puppy." He said, "Dad, if you'd just take him out for walks, he wouldn't mess up the kitchen like that."

Now as Joel talked, we were walking past several blocks of nice grass and fireplugs, but the dog showed no interest in doing anything. So Joel stopped and spoke directly to the dog. He said, "Okay, dog, *do something!*"

The dog just stared at us. He couldn't have cared less. He was waiting till he got back to the kitchen.

Then came the night of reckoning. I came home late one night after playing a bar mitzvah with my band. When I perform, I wear a toupee. Not thinking anything about either the toupee or the dog, I came home about one in the morning and wandered into the kitchen for a drink of water. The dog, evidently not recognizing me wearing the rug and thinking I was a burglar, almost ate me up. I barely managed to get out and slam the kitchen door.

Joel and Ronnie had inadvertently given me an anti-Semitic dog!

So we took the dog back to the kennel. He immediately began kissing the kennel keeper. And I broke into joyous song: "You can have him, I don't want him, he's too big for me!"

Owing to the communication problems of Joel and his family living three thousand miles away, we "have tea" on the telephone, and we send gifts on birthdays and anniversaries. When Joel and Ronnie were much younger, and I'd bring them home little deli delights, Joel would call me the Goodie Man. This year Grace and I were in a quandary over what to send Joel for his birthday, and I came up with a brainstorm.

I phoned my good friend comedian Larry Best in New York. I asked Larry to be my surrogate "Goodie" agent. I asked him to go over to the Sturgeon King Delicatessen and buy several pounds of sturgeon and corned beef and Nova Scotia salmon and a dozen bagels, get it wrapped like a gift package, and deliver it to the doorman at Joel's apartment house, enclosing a little note to Joel: "The Goodie Man is everywhere."

Two hours later Joel called us as happy as a school kid. He delightedly said, "Dad, you did it again!"

My sweetheart, Grace, and I have two wonderful sons and four wonderful grandchildren. But our courtship was a little rocky. By the time I was sixteen I was helping support my mother and father, and I was also giving my older brother, Al, a financial lift through college. So when beautiful little Gracie appeared on the scene, my family looked upon her the way chickens in a barnyard look upon a circling fox. When Grace would call up and my mother would answer the phone, the conversation would go like this:

"Hello."

"Is Mickey there?"

"Who's calling?"

"Grace."

"You've got de wrong number."

And my mother would hang up. When my father would ask who had called, my mother would say, "The vampeer"— her interpretation of a vamp, like Theda Bara.

The Epsteins, on the other hand, with five daughters, looked upon Grace's possible marital exodus with great joy. They not only would be gaining a son, but would be losing a daughter, and what's wrong with a parlay like that?

The only difficulty I had with the Epsteins was my unusual wooing hours. After a road tour with Phil Spitalny's orchestra I was playing in Doc Whipple's big band at the Golden Pheasant Chinese Restaurant in Cleveland. I finished playing at one o'clock in the morning, and I would jump into my 1927 Chevrolet and make a beeline for the Epstein home. Grace was still a high school student, and she had to get up in the morning for an early class. But since I had neither class nor principle, at one-thirty in the morning we'd head for the couch for a necking session.

Grace's father, Morris "Happy" Epstein, was in the wholesale produce business. He left for work at two A.M., which was about the time that Grace and I were warming up. Her father would come downstairs on his way out of the house. Still half asleep, he'd mutter, "Good morning kids," and walk on out the door like a zombie.

About this time Grace's mother would decide to blow the whistle on us. She'd stand at the head of the stairs and call down, "Enough already! Stop all that monkeying around! Goldie [her name for Grace when she was a young girl], you've got to get up and go to school. And you, little boy, go home and get some sleep—you're skinny like a noodle! So stop already!"

This scene was repeated almost every night.

I have loved Grace's mother for fifty years. Her humor is something special. Many of her delicious sayings I have incorporated in my act. Here's an example of her expressions. She recently came over to have dinner with us, and Grace was showing her some of her most recent artwork, including some of her new hand-painted porcelain. Grandma Fanny, in a voice filled with love and adulation, said, "Grace, it's simply gorgeous, and not bad either."

Grace's father, Happy Epstein, was an unforgettable man. He loved to dance the polka and the kazatsky. He loved pinochle and poker. Other than those few little hobbies, Happy Epstein was a devoted husband and father, a hard worker, and a good provider. He was full of life, and I loved him.

One morning after work, when I thought I'd give Grace a pass to get some sleep, I went down to the commission markets, on Woodland at Ninth, to have breakfast with Happy. His produce firm was called Epstein & Friedman (his brother-in-law). The produce stall next to them was run by the Commella brothers, who also specialized in fresh fruits and vegetables.

There was naturally a hot competition among the various

commission men when the farmers arrived with their truck-
loads of produce. The game was to grab the farmer, bid fast,
and buy. The morning I was visiting Happy a farmer drove
up with a truckload of raspberries. By the time the Commella brother on duty had finished with a customer Grace's
father had bought the entire truckload of beautiful raspberries.

Mr. Commella walked over a few minutes later and said,
"Where did he go—the farmer with the raspberries?"

Grace's father said, "I bought all the raspberries—a
hundred boxes."

Commella belligerently screamed, "Eppa-steen, you a
somana-bitch!"

Happy enthusiastically replied, "Comella, kiss by me the
ass."

In spite of this, they were friends for forty years.

Those were the days, my friend. When I was trying to
corner Grace on the sofa and her mother was outflanking
me from the top of the stairs, and Grace gradually aged
from fifteen to sixteen.

After a year with Doc Whipple's big dance band I took a
job as clarinet and sax soloist with Angelo Vitale at the
Park Theater. The Park was primarily a movie theater, but
it also had a stage revue. We played an overture, a symphonic
version of the hits of the day; at the end of the overture I
was always featured in a saxophone solo in a pin spot. We
also played for the stage revue and provided appropriate
music for the newsreels. Angelo was a beautiful little five-
foot man, with a huge head of hair which he wore in a sort
of an Italian-Afro. When he mounted the podium and
turned to lead his orchestra, the audience saw five feet of
Vitale and two feet of Vitalis.

At that time, early 1929, big orchestras—many of them
famous recording orchestras like Isham Jones, Frankie
Trumbauer, and Ben Pollack—were appearing at cafés and
ballrooms all over America. I got the jazz fever and decided
to organize a big band of my own.

I started assembling some of Cleveland's finest dance
musicians. At the same time a Chinese restaurant owner
named George Louie was opening a big new Chinese
restaurant called the Piccadilly, at Twentieth and Euclid.
We auditioned for George, and he said, "Kat, I like you.
You hired."

The first two months business was good; then came the
'29 crash, and the Piccadilly became Cleveland's first empty
Chinese restaurant. Everybody enjoyed our music except
one little Chinese waiter. I don't think he liked my singing.
One night after I'd done my jazzy vocal on "Button Up
Your Overcoat," he put a note on my music stand in Chinese-
type English letters saying, "Maggie Kat, you sing like cow.
Please cut out."

And George Louie's final fortune cookie, just before his
historic Declaration of Bankruptcy, was his saying to me,
"Kat, you got great band. When you can go, please?"

That finished me and my big band. I decided to head for
New York, the land of milk and money.

But before leaving Cleveland, I gave my sweet Grace an
engagement ring, while I could still afford it. This inspired
her parents to throw an unforgettable engagement party
to celebrate. The Epstein house on Eighty-fifth Street was
packed with the Epstein and the Katz Klans. With the
difference in the families' views, the atmosphere could
hardly have been chillier if Grace had been a *shiksa* (non-
Jewish). My folks sat on one side of the room, hers on the
other, staring across no-man's-land at each other.

On the dining-room table were great platters of chopped
liver, herring, *ptcha,* and other Jewish delicacies. But nobody was touching a bite—my folks weren't ready to sur-
render yet. Then Mrs. Epstein suddenly stood up and
loudly proclaimed, "Everybody, let's go to the table! Eat
and be happy!"

As the two sides approached the table Grace's father was
ready with the vishnik, the homemade Russian cherry
brandy. The Russians have always had the atomic bomb;

they just call it vishnik. After drinking a few glasses, the party relaxed to the point of mazel tovs on all sides, mutual blessings, happy pledges of eternal friendship, and a mass attack on the chopped liver. Happy Epstein stood at one side of the revelry, glass on high, singing, "Life is just a bowl of vishnik!"

Later on, after the cookies, the Epsteins served Seidlitz powders, the Rolaids of the late twenties.

Many top musicians in Cleveland came to my engagement party. They included a young fellow clarinetist named Artie Shaw, who at the time was playing saxophone and clarinet in Austin Wylie's orchestra at the Golden Pheasant. Artie hadn't yet Begun the Beguine, but he was already a terrific clarinetist and a fine arranger.

Two days later I left on the morning train for New York, for a solo shot at fame and fortune. I had $100, in cash, and my clarinet and alto sax. And a size 30 tuxedo, with Skinner's satin lapels.

2 · A Kitten Is Born

MEYER MYRON "Mickey" Katz was born on June 15, 1909, on a little street on the east side of Cleveland named Sawtelle Court. I have been waiting for the city to mark the site with some sort of modest plaque—possibly a life-size bust in chicken liver by the noted sculptor Jacob Epstein—but so far nothing. All that is known is that my birthplace was near Fifty-first and Woodland Avenue, which was near "the gully." At our tiny house on Sawtelle Court we were very poor, but we had each other.

The term "melting pot" was coined to describe the early-twentieth-century Cleveland into which I was born. It was a city of maybe seven hundred thousand people, and it was one of America's first conglomerates. Boy oh boy, were we conglomerated! Irish, Italians, Jews, Poles, blacks, Croatians, Lithuanians, Slovenians, Yugoslavians, Greeks, Russians—Cleveland had 'em all! Maybe that's why I've always had a feeling of tolerance for others.

The neighborhood where I was born was not a tenement-row area like New York's Lower East Side. Around 1909 the Jewish immigrants in Cleveland lived in areas of tiny individual houses or in tiny apartments and flats, often in the rear of a little grocery or candy store. The grocery was where poor people bought food if they could delay payment till Tuesday, and the candy store was where everybody met socially. Many early racketeers met at these little candy stores, and some of them were killed there.

Many kittens open their eyes to face a harsh world. So did I. My first childhood memory is of being maybe four years old and standing with my father outside an ancient gray wooden structure—a real apparition of a sanitarium—near Fifty-seventh and Outhwaite. After a moment my father said, "Mama's in there."

As I found out later, my mother had suffered a total breakdown and had to be in this sanitarium for three months because of the tragic death of my older sister Tilly, who had died of diphtheria when she was nine. My mother must have sensed that in a few more years deaths from diphtheria would be needless; she couldn't accept the blow of Tilly's death. It was such a total shock to my mother that she lost most of her hair while she was in the sanitarium, and even after we brought her home, the family never told her where Tilly was buried.

But I learned much later about this tragedy. All I knew as I stood outside the ugly old sanitarium with my father was that somehow my mother had been taken away from me, and I wondered if I'd ever see Mama again.

After my mother was released from the sanitarium, we all moved in with my grandmother and grandfather, and without them I don't know what we would have done.

My mother was an educated woman. She grew up in Libau, Latvia, where her father was a bookbinder. She went to the local high school, called a Gymnasium, where she was taught by German professors. When she was still a girl, my mother spoke several languages: German, Latvian, and Yiddish.

On the other hand, my father in neighboring Lithuania had no schooling at all. Our family joke about my father was that he'd got out of Europe just before the Russians got him by the Baltics.

But before leaving Europe, my father stopped in Latvia long enough to marry my mother. She was four years older than my father. Their marriage was arranged by a *shadchen,* a marriage broker, as in *Fiddler on the Roof.*

My mother and father both had delicious senses of humor. In those cold Cleveland winters, when I was growing up, my mother never had a decent winter coat that I can remember. Later, when she saw a friend wearing a cheap rabbit-fur job that must have cost all of thirty bucks, she forever afterward spoke of her as "Mrs. Tenenzweig, the society lady."

Here are a couple more of Mama's conversational pearls. When a lady would walk by who was well endowed—and well reared—my mother would describe her as "a comfortable woman." In speaking of her bachelor brother, Mama said, "Sam's a millionaire—he's got five thousand dollars."

The only training for making a living that my father had received in the old country was as a tailor's apprentice. When he first came to Cleveland, before he had various little tailor shops of his own, he worked for established tailoring firms. One of the most notable was Hickling Brothers, downtown on Euclid Avenue, which made suits for the ultrarich. One of my father's proud boasts was that Hickling Brothers had once made a suit for John D. Rockefeller, Sr., who, like me, had grown up in Cleveland. (That's where our similarity ended.)

For a time, after my mother came home from the sanitarium, my father ran a little grocery store so that he could be near home to help take care of Mama. But my father was not much of a businessman. He extended credit to everybody, especially people who didn't pay. He shortly had such a grateful clientele that he went out of business.

There was a scarcity of sugar during World War I. You'd have to pay a sugar bootlegger $20 for a sack. One night Papa put me on a sled and we sloshed six blocks through the snow to East Sixty-first Street and Quincy Avenue, where in a barn a sugar bootlegger loaded a twenty-pound sack of sugar on the sled, grabbed my poor Papa's $20 and we sloshed back home.

With a different start in life, my father, instead of being a poor tailor, could have been a great musician. He loved classical music. To him Jascha Heifetz was a "jin-us" (a genius). "He's got plenty tech [technique] on the wiolin." In later years just to see what he'd say, I once asked him, "How do you think Heifetz compares with Mischa Elman?"

He didn't hesitate a second. "Mischa Elman's got the tone; Heifetz has got the tech." And I want to tell you: Papa was right!

Papa also loved opera. He was crazy about "Galla-coochie" (Galli-Curci) and "Ca-roosel" (Caruso). "He's got a woice."

My father knew radio and movie personalities by *his* names for them. And he unconsciously gave Jewish names to any actor he admired. Clifton Fadiman became Clifton Fetterman. Lauren Bacall became Lauren Bagel. Any actor whose name he didn't know at all he described. James Cagney was the Tough Guy. Robert Taylor was the *shayner* (the handsome one). One night late in his life my father was watching a film of Humphrey Bogart on TV. Excitedly he turned to me and said, "This is the best actor from everybody!"

Joking with him, I said, "Papa, what's his name?"

"You don't know?"

"No, Papa."

"For God's sake, he was the Queen of Africa!"

When I was a little boy, I was, oddly enough, a quiet little fellow. But in those days kids had to "do something to help the family." So at age eight I tried selling newspapers. That lasted two days. On the second day I came home frozen like a popsicle. But financially I had cleaned up—I had made a dime. My next job was cleaning up Uncle Bernhart's grocery store.

Then I became a chewing-gum magnate. By this time

we had moved to Outhwaite Avenue, and a man who ran a candy store there hired little kids to sell chewing gum for him on consignment. If you sold a whole box of gum, you made twenty-four cents. But it was slow going.

Till I got an idea. There were two poolrooms across the street from each other at Fifty-fifth and Woodland. One was Haltnorth Billiards, and across the street was the Ideal Billiards. Many gamblers and gangsters used these two pool-rooms as hangouts.

There was a lot of gambling that went on around Cleveland when I was a young lad. The small-time gambling went on in the back rooms of barbershops and phony tobacco-store fronts—places like the Kibitzers. Here suckers trying to make it the easy way would play card games like "stush." They'd usually lose, but win or lose, the gangsters would pick up a surefire percentage of the money as it went by. If the cops came in, the barber or the tobacco-store man would give a signal, and when the cops would break in the door to the back room, there was no sign of any gambling.

And while I am talking about neighborhood gambling hideaways, here's a story: A few years later, when I was a young teenager, the Jewish community, including the Katz family, had moved up to One Hundred and Fifth Street. There was a little old cantor there who used to drive an equally old Model T Ford. He was about four feet eleven inches tall, and he had a beard that reached to his *pupik* (his navel). When the kids would see him coming in his old Model T, they'd say, "Here comes the driverless Ford."

Anyway, one day down One Hundred and Fifth Street came old man Berkowitz, the little cantor. This day, no doubt thinking about something else, he ran through the red traffic light at the corner, and because of his panic over that, he drove up on the curb, across the sidewalk, and right in through the glass front of a cigar store with gambling in the back. The huge Hungarian who owned the place walked over and looked down at little frightened Berkowitz, sitting in the middle of the smashed cigar store in his Model T. The big Hungarian roared, "You Russian *basssssssssssstard*, you!" The terrified little cantor didn't know what to say, so he looked up and said, "You hunky monkey, dot's what you are."

When I was a small boy, I knew that the hotshot hoodlums gathered at the two pool halls at the corner of Fifty-fifth and Woodland. And I figured that they wouldn't want a lot of attention called to them by a punk kid standing out in front loudly peddling chewing gum. So I got a box of chewing gum on consignment from the candy-store man and hightailed it over to the nearest of the two pool halls. I stationed myself out in front and began "selling" my wares in as loud a voice as possible.

As I had figured, the first racketeer who came along said, "Hey, punk, what are you doing here?" He snatched the box of gum out of my hand, tossed me a dollar, and said, "Now get the hell out of here, you little shit!"

I took the dollar, went back to the candy store, got another box of gum, and stationed myself in front of the other pool hall across the street. In a few minutes, the same result: another dollar.

Unfortunately, this chewing-gum bonanza lasted only a few days. One afternoon after school I had just arrived in front of one of the pool halls with a fresh supply of gum when a gangland character not six feet away got shot right through the head and rolled into the gutter in a pool of blood, dead. I ran home crying and told my mother what had happened, and that ended my chewing-gum business. Mama said, "Keep away from the bums."

By the time I was eleven I knew that I wanted to be a musician. I also knew that I wanted to play the clarinet.

That reminds me of another happening of my childhood. One night all the family—or as many as could get in—were gathered for a party at my Uncle Charley's. In the middle of the party I and a couple of my cousins—we were aged eight to ten—locked ourselves in the bathroom because there was no other place in the tiny crowded apartment where little boys could have any privacy to talk. But Uncle Charley soon knocked on the door till we opened it, and he gave us a short lecture. He said, "Boys, don't pull on it, or you'll get brain fever."

I ran into one of those same cousins—my Cousin Bernie— just the other day. He's now one of the country's top commercial artists. I said, "Bernie, you look great! You never got brain fever, huh?"

He said, "No, how about you?"

Now back to the clarinet. One night when I was eleven, my father took me to a concert at the Talmud Torah (the Hebrew school). The tickets for these concerts cost ten cents for adults and five cents for children. In my case it was a close decision, but Papa managed to get me in for five cents.

It was the most magical night of my life. Sitting in the darkened auditorium, I heard a clarinet solo played by a talented teenager named Leo Levin. (Leo was to become a great doctor in Cleveland and Miami Beach, my friend for fifty years, and the doctor who one night performed an emergency appendectomy on my son Joel. I will never forget Leo Levin.)

The night I first heard Leo he was fourteen years old. He played the "Shadow Song" from *Dinorah,* by Meyerbeer. I remember every moment of that evening. It decided the course of my life. On the way home I said, "Papa, I want to play the clarinet."

My father thought that was fine, but we had no money either to buy a clarinet or to pay for any lessons. Al with his violin, my sister Jeanne with her piano, and little Estelle with her dancing lessons were already keeping Papa broke. There simply wasn't any additional clarinet money. I had unfortunately come in last on the Katz musical totem pole.

But there had to be a way. By this time I was going to Central Junior High, which was in the same building with Central Senior High, which had a forty-piece band. The next afternoon I stood outside Room 451, the band room, listening to the band practice, like a starving boy looking through the window of a deli at a mound of *kishka* (sausagelike meat, flour, and spices).

When the band practice was over, I got up enough courage to ask bandmaster Harry Clark if there was by any chance a school clarinet available. There must have been something in the way I said it that induced him to say that he'd look around. A few days later he handed me a dusty and ancient clarinet that had evidently been carried by some luckless soldier-musician during the Spanish-American War. I kid you not. It had "United States Government—1898" stamped on it.

I carried it home as though it were a kosher version of the Holy Grail. It was a clarinet! And, at least temporarily, it was mine!

All I needed now was a teacher. Harry Clark said that the finest clarinet teacher in Cleveland was an old Bohemian professor named Joseph Narovec. I took two streetcars— the Cedar Avenue and then the West Twenty-fifth Street —clear across town to see him at the West Side School of Music.

Today I worship at Joseph Narovec's shrine. He was the only clarinet teacher I ever had. He was six feet six inches tall, which in those days was simply incredible. I felt as if he were standing on a ladder and I were standing in a hole. He had a big mustache and looked like Emperor Franz Joseph. His clarinet lessons, he said, cost a dollar and a half. Which I, of course, didn't have. And I knew of no place to get it.

Till I thought of Uncle Sam—my Jewish Uncle Sam—who had a tiny tailor shop where he also sold used clothing. Uncle Sam was a bachelor and had no family responsibilities. Also, he stayed open six days a week, including Saturday, the Sabbath—my father called him a goy (a gentile).

I went to see Uncle Sam. I told him that I would come over every Saturday morning and clean up his little tailor shop if he would give me the dollar and a half a week for my clarinet lessons. He said, "Meyer, it's okay by me." (Meyer was my maiden name.)

Uncle Sam not only paid for my first clarinet lessons, but gave me one of my first lessons in sex. I don't mean sax sex —or little-boys-in-the-bathroom sex—I mean de real sex. One Saturday morning I went over there as usual; his shop blinds were still drawn, and there was no sign of life around the joint. I pounded on the door repeatedly. And just as I was about to run home and tell my mother that Sam must be ill, the door opened and out came Uncle Sam, preceded by a well-stacked female. "Hello, Meyer," said Uncle Sam. "Was that you knocking on the door while I was giving this lady a fitting?"

Those Saturday morning sessions were something to remember. After three months of lessons and practice my uncle thought I was a genius already. So he started inviting his business neighbors and other friends in to hear me play. He would proudly sit cross-legged on his sewing table, and he would say, "Meyer, play me a 'Yankee Doodle.'"

So I would play "Yankee Doodle." Then my uncle would ask the audience for requests. The audience included auctioneers, bookies, and racetrack touts—Uncle Sam was *meshuga* (crazy) for the ponies. These sporty characters came up with such odd requests as "Believe Me If All Those Endearing Young Charms," "The Second Hungarian Rhapsody," and "The Last Rose of Summer." The ones I didn't know I faked. In a few months, oh, boy, did I have a repertoire. Hoo-ha!

I was also becoming a recognized musician at home. After six months I could play all sorts of legitimate music, and I could fake all the hit tunes of the day. With my brother, Al, on violin (in those days he was Abe), my sister Jeanne on piano, and with Estelle's lovely voice, we began to have family concerts. By this time we had moved up in class to four rooms back of Papa's first personally owned little tailor shop at Seventy-fourth and Cedar.

To finance the new shop, Papa had taken the day coach to Bridgeport, Connecticut, and borrowed $50 from a dozen cousins. After he got home, he discovered that he needed another $50, but he managed to finance this other half locally, from uncles. Papa spent most of his combined capital for a Prosperity Pressing Machine—a great steam-spewing monster. When he first got it installed and fired it up, it exploded three times. Even after he got it running right, when you went into the tailor shop it was usually difficult to see Papa among the clouds of steam.

We began our family concerts in the summer. Being Cleveland, it was hot, and when we got together in the living room on Saturday nights to play and sing, we'd open the apartment windows and the curtains to get some air. It was with some surprise that we began to notice that when we'd finish, there would be forty or fifty people standing outside in the street, listening to our music. Later we learned that the neighbors referred to our Saturday night concerts as Katz's Follies.

In those days amateur nights were the rage at the neighborhood theaters. They'd present eight or ten amateur acts, and the act receiving the most applause would get the grand prize of $2 or $3. If two acts tied in the applause, they'd split the prize. If it was an unusually full house and the management felt generous, it might make it a $5 GRAND PRIZE.

When I was about twelve, my younger sister Estelle and I decided through necessity that we were professional enough for amateur nights.

At the theaters we'd pretend that we didn't know each other. My sister was introduced as Estelle Kay—she was ten —she would come onstage and do a great song and dance, with our sister Jeannie playing piano for her, and the audience would go crazy. She was a beautiful child and superbly talented.

A few acts later Myron Katz would fly onstage, point his licorice stick high in the air, and blow the pants off "St.

Louis Blues"—and the audience would flip all over again.

Three amateur nights out of four Estelle and I would end up tied for the first prize. We'd split the loot—publicly —then hurry home and give it all to Mama so she could buy some groceries. There was only one thing that sometimes went wrong. Occasionally the top prize would be a five-pound box of candy—and how do you split that? Also, if there was one thing we didn't need at home, it was a five-pound box of candy.

But we solved that, too. I'd garner more applause by grandly giving the box of candy to Estelle: "She's a little girl, sweets to the sweet." Then after the show Estelle would stand out in front of the theater in her little ballet costume that my mother and father had hand-sewn for her, and like a little English flower girl, she'd call out to those leaving the theater, "Would anyone like to buy my candy?" She'd sell the five-pound box of candy for a couple of dollars, and we'd go home with cash.

We did that many and many a night.

When I was fifteen, I was ready to become a professional musician. With the encouragement of my teacher, Joseph Narovec, I had joined the Musicians Union and had bought a better clarinet, and a sax, on credit from Herman Wodicka, who had a music store on Huron Road.

Deciding that I was ready to enter the adult musical world, Mr. Narovec went to see his old friend Henry Newman, the manager of the Johnston Society Orchestras. As I learned later, Narovec told him, "Henry, you come from poor parents. I'm a man from the old country. Here's a boy who's a good musician. No matter how young he is, he's a great player. Please give him a chance."

The next day I got a call from Henry Newman. He said, "Mr. Narovec told me all about you. You're hired for Saturday night."

I was a hit on my opening night—and made five bucks! From then on I was a regular with the Johnston Society Orchestras.

I also played some highly *non*society jobs. Mr. Newman called one afternoon. Did I have a pair of white pants? I didn't, but my father had a pair I could borrow. Newman said, "Good, go out to Broadview Road Saturday night to a roadhouse out there called the Broadview Inn. The job starts at eight o'clock."

What took place that Saturday night at the Broadview Inn was a stag party. Our three-piece orchestra played while a naked broad was out on the floor making with the bumps and the grinds. My temperature was going up, and so was something else. That night I became a man, two years after my bar mitzvah.

There was another memorable occasion with the Johnston orchestra, this time *with* society hoi polloi goys. I mention it to show you how the country club crowd can piss away their money.

There was one country club in Cleveland called, with simple elegance, the Country Club. It was one of many "restricted" clubs in Cleveland. We used to say that the restrictions included Jews, Catholics, shanty Irish, Poles, Chinese, Japanese, and Arabian horses. The Country Club was away out past the Heights, and it was where many of the zillionaires belonged. One night, when we were playing there a young man came up to the bandstand and said to Jimmy Johnston, "That little fellow who plays the clarinet . . . I'd like to hire him, your trumpet player, and your drummer. I want them out on the first tee Sunday morning at six-thirty."

Here was the gag. This guy had invited a rich friend to come out from New York and play a round of golf with him and his friends. The New Yorker got in on Saturday night, they picked him up and wined and dined him, got him drunk as a lord, took him to several whorehouses, and Sunday morning they poured the poor son of a bitch into his golf clothes and got him out on the course at six-thirty. They told him it was the only starting time they could get.

Well, the three of us musicians were hiding back of a big

bush with our instruments. As the poor hung-over guy
started to swing to tee off, we shattered what was left of his
nerves by suddenly blasting away on "HAPPY DAYS ARE
HERE AGAIN!" We played a dozen notes—LOUD ONES
—took our five bucks apiece, and went home. I guess they
took the guy to the booby hatch. Rich or poor, it's nice to
have money.

Now all this time I was also going to high school, good old
Central High. It was a beautiful school; at least I thought
so at the time. It was the oldest high school west of the
Alleghenies. We had a melting-pot student body, the
majority of whom were Jews, Italians, and blacks.

We didn't even have an athletic field at Central. The
teams practiced in the schoolyard, which was gravel and
asphalt. If you broke a football shoulder pad, you didn't get
another one—the school didn't have another one. If you
broke your leg, the school couldn't get you another one of
those either. My only connection with the football team was
serving as water boy and playing in the band, such as it was.
When we played uptown at Cathedral Latin, the great
Catholic high school, its band would come marching down
the field in beautiful striped uniforms, with the big plumed
hats. Then our band would come marching along in whatever pieces of uniform we could find—one kid in a pair of
his father's yellow pants, another kid in a coat with brass
buttons he'd found somewhere. We were the damnedest-
looking high school band the world has ever seen. But
we played well.

At Central High we also had an ROTC unit—the Reserve
Officers Training Corps—that should not be denied its place
in history. Sergeant Riley, a dedicated Army man, did his
best to direct and train our ROTC unit, but we remained
a sad sack outfit. We just couldn't seem to get the hang of
drilling. In those days all the Cleveland high school ROTC
units had an annual military review at Gordon Park. After
our annual appearances Sergeant Riley was usually found in
the park later in the day, weeping. One year there was a big

mud puddle in Gordon Park; we, of course, marched right
into it. Since we all were rather short, we gradually disap-
peared. Shortly after that Sergeant Riley joined the Navy.

We'd never had much of a football team, but after football great Frank Civiletto, who had been graduated from
Central High, returned to his alma mater as coach, we beat
some of the biggest and richest schools in town. Since they
were understandably resentful, very few of us ventured
across town to the games to cheer for the good old Red-and-
Blue. (Our school colors should have been Black-and-Blue.)

Central's cheering section at the games across town often
consisted only of me and my friend Wizzle Rosenberg.
Wizzle was a trumpet player in the band, and he was the
original Mr. Five-by-Five. He was a heavyset, powerful kid.
I weighed in at about ninety-three pounds, but any time
any bigger kids would want to beat me up Wizzle would
kick the hell out of them. Later he played trumpet with me
in my band; one night when we were walking down Huron
Road somebody made an anti-Semitic crack, and Wizzle
threw him through a plate-glass window.

But even with Wizzle along, going to the high school
games across town wasn't any picnic. At one important
football game our team beat a tough West Side school, and
while Wizzle and I were loudly cheering—a cheering section
of two—we saw a whole bunch of rival students heading for
us with mayhem on their minds. We ran for the locker
room, and Frank Civiletto got us safely inside with the team
and locked the door. We all stayed there till the police
arrived in three big Peerless cars and "rode shotgun" for us
till they got us safely on the streetcar headed for home. At
Central High we had no team buses. Our football and
basketball teams rode the streetcar across town to play the
other schools.

We had one "racial incident" at Central High that I
remember. Not among the students—we got along fine—but
with the faculty. (The reason the racial hodgepodge of
students got along was that we had one thing in common—

poverty.) On Friday afternoons we had school dances on the first floor. Miss Whitmore, a huge lady, would play the piano, and I would stand alongside her and alternate on clarinet and sax. One Friday afternoon when we were playing our usual "exciting" dance music, such numbers as "I Want to Be Happy," "Rosalie," and "Who?" from *Sunny,* a black youngster asked a white girl standing next to him if she'd like to dance. She said fine, and they started dancing together. That lasted about four seconds, till our vice-principal could charge over there. He grabbed the boy and said, "The colors don't blend. Please get off the floor." That was fifty years ago, but I can still see the look on that boy's face, reflecting his frustration and misery.

Maybe that was part of why I continued going to Central High till I graduated. By the time I was a senior we had moved "uptown" to a better neighborhood. I was making $70 a week with the clarinet and sax, and my father was doing a little better with the tailoring, so we moved from Cedar Avenue up to a duplex on Glenville Avenue, near the lakefront. It was also near One Hundred and Fifth Street, which was the new center of the Jewish community; my father had opened a shop at One Hundred and Fifth and Ostend Avenue; it was called Max Katz, The Family Tailor.

All the kids in the new neighborhood went to the new school—Glenville High—but I took two streetcars back and forth every day in order to continue going to Central. I was president of the Central High senior class, an honor student, water boy for the football team, president of the band and glee club. Also, Central made a unique effort to cooperate with my unusual working hours. I would get home about one o'clock in the morning, after working at various gin mills, and there was no way in this world that I could be at school at eight o'clock. My senior year in high school I weighed about as much as a feather from a small duck, and I was groggy most of the time from lack of sleep. The only thing that saved me was that my teachers at Central High, since my grades were good, passed a special ruling that Mickey Katz could come to school every morning not at eight o'clock, but at ten o'clock. Central High was good to me, and I loved Central High.

But I must finish telling you about my powerful buddy Wizzle Rosenberg. We went to high school together fifty years ago, but we still write each other. He became a great trumpet player, and today he plays the bugle for the post parade at the two Cleveland racetracks—Thistledown and Cranwood. He has also become a dealer and expert in rare recordings.

But I really wanted to tell you some more not about Wizzle, but about his parents. His father was blind; but he had a terrific sense of humor, and he composed all sorts of songs—popular songs, Jewish songs. He'd get his songs printed up into sheet music and go around selling them for ten cents a copy.

When he wasn't writing songs, he'd help Wizzle's mother run a small grocery store they had on Quincy Avenue. In those days you got herring and pickles not out of a jar, but out of a barrel. Mrs. Rosenberg always wore "protective cuffs"—sheets of newspaper fastened with rubber bands— for the ladies who would come in and say they'd like a herring. She would look into the herring barrel and hopefully ask, "How about that nice one there on top?" The ladies would always say, "No, I'd like one a little foider down." So she'd have to dive to the bottom of the barrel to get the requested herring.

The same mishmosh went on with the pickles.

I also don't want to forget to tell you about Katz's mice. We had moved from 5908 Outhwaite Avenue to 2155 Seventy-fourth Street, at the corner of Cedar. We lived there for about four years. This flat had a tiny living room, a tiny kitchen, and two tiny bedrooms. Papa and Mama slept in one bedroom, my two sisters slept in the other one, and my brother, Al, and I slept in the living room on a sofa. It was so cold in winter that if we had any coal, we'd keep the

fireplace going all night, and in the morning the mice
would be clustered around the fireplace keeping warm. Papa
would get up early and come through the living room to go
open the tailor shop, which was in front, and when he'd
see the mice, he'd go berserk. He'd snatch off one of his
shoes and start beating at them and chasing them. But
the mice always won; the next morning they were back,
ready for another gig. Finally, Papa got some traps, and we
got rid of the mice. I think I missed them. The fireplace
looked a little lonely.

Now before I finish my childhood tales, I want to tell you
about *Shabbes* (the Sabbath) at our house. This sweet
memory will be in my heart as long as I live.

The Sabbath is, of course, from sundown Friday to sundown Saturday, and Friday was always spent getting ready
for *Shabbes*. My mother would do all the cooking; then she
would wash all the floors by hand and put papers all over
the clean kitchen floor. The popular Yiddish paper was the
Jewish Daily Forward, which was published in New York
and sold all over the country. After it was read, it was used
to cover the floor. As comedian Phil Foster says about his
own mother, "Every Friday we had wall-to-wall *Forwards.*"

With the kitchen floor clean, Mama would next make
gribbenes (grib-uh-ness), little pieces of chicken skin fried
crisp. For us kids, the greatest thing in the world was to
come home from school on Friday afternoons and have a
few pieces of *gribbenes*—otherwise known as Jewish pop-
corn.

Then my mother would make the sponge cake and put it
in the oven. I remember one Friday afternoon when I came
home and banged the door and my mother went rushing to
the kitchen, crying, *"Oy vay,* the sponge cake fell down!"

When Papa got home, he took his bath, got dressed, and
went to the synagogue. In Orthodox synagogues this would
usually be a short service, presided over not by the rabbi,
but by the cantor. Papa would come home around seven-
thirty, and he would recite the *kiddush* (the blessing) over

the wine and another prayer over the *challa* (the loaf of twisted egg bread).

Then my mother started serving the dinner. There would be matzo ball soup, maybe with *kreplach* (Jewish ravioli) in it. There would be gefilte fish and the chicken. We'd also have *chrayn* (red horseradish). And we'd finish with "compote"—any sort of stewed fruit we had—and the sponge cake.

No matter how sparse the menu might be the rest of the week, on Friday nights we *ate;* oh, did we eat! We kids always looked forward to the Sabbath; our little stomachs just purred.

Comedian Marty Drake tells a wonderful true story about his family's Friday night *Shabbes* meal. His mother did a brisk business in free meals. They lived directly across the street from a little synagogue, and Marty's father would bring needy strangers home with him for dinner. As a result, she never knew what would be left for her five children till she looked out the window and saw how many strangers Papa was bringing home.

On this particular Sabbath Marty's mother had cooked one small chicken. When she looked out the window, here came Papa with four freeloaders from the *shul* (synagogue).

She turned to her children and said, "Kids, Papa's coming with four freeloaders, and we've only got one chicken. So when I say, 'Who wants chicken?' please, children, say, 'I don't want chicken.' "

Papa came in with his four guests, everybody sat down at the table, and Mama said, "Who wants chicken?"

The kids all dutifully said, "I don't want chicken." And they sat there with their little tongues hanging out while the four guests devoured the chicken.

Then she brought out the one small apple cake she'd baked and asked, "Who wants apple cake?"

The kids, not having been coached on this, all said, "I'll take apple cake!"

Marty's mother, thinking quickly, said, "Those that

didn't want chicken can't have any apple cake."

Saturday morning my father, my older brother, and I would go to the synagogue. This was a full service. We would come home, have our lunch, and Papa would take a nap. This was his Saturday afternoon routine. The fact that he might not possess worldly goods disturbed him not at all. *Shabbes* was *Shabbes*. After a nap of a couple of hours my father would get up and go back to the synagogue for the late-afternoon service.

Papa's observance of the *Shabbes* didn't help his income. Seventy-fourth and Cedar, where we lived at the time, was a predominantly Irish neighborhood. The Irish Catholics wanted their clothes mended and pressed on Saturday, so they could dress up for church on Sunday. But my father, an Orthodox Jew, remained closed on Saturday. At first business in his little tailor shop was terrible. But gradually some of the Irish people began to respect him for his staunch observance of his religion, and they began bringing in their clothes other days of the week. Not enough to make a decent living, but enough to enable Papa to devote his *Shabbes* to solitude and prayer.

Much of my mother's deep religious feelings were expressed in doing things for others. My mother had her own charities: She would salvage portions of food from our meals; she would find items of clothing here and there. All the time I was a little boy I remember my mother packing up food or clothes in a basket and taking several streetcars clear across town to help someone less fortunate than we were.

My wonderful mother, if you please, was also a would-be stage actress. Some fifteen miles east out of Cleveland, on the south shore of Lake Erie, was a place called Camp Wise. It was a summer camp for poor Jewish youngsters, supported by Jewish and non-Jewish charities. In the heat of the Cleveland summers a kid from six to twelve could go to Camp Wise for a week of fresh air, good food, and fun for practically nothing.

A half mile away on the same campgrounds was a special section called Mothers' Camp (supported by the Council Educational Alliance) for mothers and small children. My mother and my sisters Jeanne and Estelle went there for years.

And that's where Mama had a chance to be onstage. My sister Jeanne wrote and produced many plays there and directed plays by others. One of the plays that Jeanne directed was an old Russian play, called *Yeckele's Krechmer* (which means "Yeckele the Innkeeper"). My mother, since there was a shortage of male actors, starred in the role of the innkeeper.

In the play Mama was dressed like a typical Russian innkeeper—in men's clothes, with a full black beard and a derby hat. In later years Jeanne showed Joel a picture of my mother in this male costume. Joel said, "No wonder I'm mixed up—my grandmother was my grandfather!"

Finally, I can't leave my childhood without telling you about my own beloved grandfather, Mama's father. His name was Joseph Herzberg (my mother's maiden name was Johanna Herzberg). He and my Uncle Isadore Herzberg, who today is ninety-one years old and living in good health and handsome retirement in Phoenix, opened a monument business in Cleveland called Joseph Herzberg & Son, Monuments. My grandfather had a standard joke; when anybody would ask him how business was, he would say, "Lead."

Their business sign out in front was in English on one side and in Yiddish on the other. My Uncle Izzy was the business head; he went to Vermont once a year to buy the marble for the monuments, and he would handle the sales contracts with the customers. My grandfather, who was then in his sixties, would take down all the facts in Yiddish, then he'd painstakingly carve the tombstones with a hand chisel. More often than not, the customers would pay the $75 in installments—$20 down and $10 or $20 a month.

For many years Joseph Herzberg & Son was the leading monument maker for the Jewish community. The business was begun in a little stoneyard at Twenty-second and Woodland; then it was moved up to Fifty-ninth and Woodland, then finally to One Hundred and Fifth and Superior, which was the last place Grandpa worked.

During his lifetime Grandpa was the eyes and ears—and the heart—of the family. He was sensitive to the troubles and travails of all of us. My mother and her sisters were very poor. When things were unusually bad, they'd go to see Grandpa. All they had to do was start by saying, "Papa . . ." and out would come his little purse with a crumpled dollar or two. Grandpa was a wonderful man.

He was only five feet tall. He used to hook one leg over the other, and on his free foot he'd swing little Estelle up and down as he'd call out, *"Hinza heidza, hop-pop-pah!"* All the grandchildren thought they were on a wonderful merry-go-round.

After my grandmother died, Grandpa lived with us for many years as an important member of our household. There were times when my father thought that Grandpa was too important a member of our household; at the Passover seders my grandfather, being the oldest male member of the family, thought that he should preside at the head of the table instead of my father. They finally compromised by both sitting at the head of the table, with the traditional pillows at their backs, and presiding together.

To this day I miss my grandfather.

How he died was typical of his life. When he was eighty-four, an old cantor friend of his lost a leg in an accident. When the man came home from the hospital, Grandpa decided to go visit him and give him a few dollars. It was a bitterly cold night. Upon leaving the cantor's house, Grandpa slipped on the icy steps and fractured his skull. He died two weeks later.

The day Grandpa was buried I stood outside the funeral home with my father. Papa was not only a very devout man, but also a *kohen* (ko-hane), claiming descent from the high priests of ancient Israel. And according to my father, since

I was the son of a *kohen,* there were certain things that I dare not do. One was that unless the deceased was your immediate family—your father or mother or brother or sister or child—you were not supposed to look upon the dead. My older brother, Al, rebelled and went inside with the rest of the family and the other mourners. I stood outside with my father, instead of being inside to say goodby to my beloved *zayde* (grandpa).

At important religious functions, such as High Holy Days at the synagogue, my father and the other *kohanim* prayed in a special way—with both hands extended, the thumbs touching, the tips of the next two fingers touching, and the last two fingers together.

I've dwelled on this in order to tell you a true story. Two years later, when Joel was three weeks old, Grace and I bundled him up and took him across town for his first trip to visit his grandparents. When I uncovered the basket to display our son to my papa and mama, there was little Joel with his hands extended in perfect *kohen* prayer fashion— the tips of his tiny thumbs together, the next two fingers together, and the last two fingers pressed together.

Well, this was almost too much for my father. He thought that Joel had been sent straight from heaven. Even at the age of three weeks, Joel was a smash hit.

3 · Worms in the Big Apple

Or

Oy Vay-It's Louis & Kay!

ON MY FOURTEEN-HOUR TRAIN RIDE to New York, I was thus thinking about my past, present, and future. Then suddenly it was midnight and the train was pulling into big, bustling Grand Central Station. I was in New York, where, God willing, I'd knock 'em dead.

To make my father feel that he was part of my expedition, I had asked his advice on a New York hotel. He didn't know any more about New York than I did, but in his *Daily Forward* he'd seen ads for a hotel called Libby's. He said, "When you get to New York, go to Libby's Hotel."

When the cabdriver said, "Where to?" and I said, "Libby's," he said, "You're kidding."

"That's where Papa said to go."

"Then Papa was kidding."

But I insisted, and off we went to Libby's, Papa's kosher hostelry. It was at Delancey and Essex, in the center of the Lower East Side. The next morning I was awakened by the loudest cacophony I have ever heard in my life. I looked out the window, and below in the street there must have been five hundred pushcarts, with the peddlers all yelling, "BAGELS! . . . COATS! . . . DRESSES! . . . UM-

BRELLAS! . . . SAFETY PINS!" It was a sight never to be forgotten. It was the heyday of the Lower East Side.

Libby's wasn't primarily a hotel; it was essentially a concrete *shvitz* (bathhouse). When I'd checked in the night before, I thought the rate seemed high—$2.50 a day—but the clerk proudly explained that this included "the baths." So on my first morning I wrapped a sheet around me, took the elevator down to the basement, and tried "the baths." This feature of the hotel consisted of huge Russians laying you on a marble slab and beating the hell out of you with their big hands and with big brooms soaked in hot soapy water.

After my first battering in the bathhouse I decided that I didn't need being that clean. Surviving Libby's baths was, in two words, "tzum-possible."

My next move was to the East Bronx, where I took a room with an elderly cousin of Grace's mother, Mrs. Treine Miller. (I had my "Mrs. Miller" long before Merv Griffin got his.) The room was tiny, but Cousin Treine charged me only $3 a week. It was on Tiffany Street, an area of very swanky garbage. When I looked out the window of my room, I had a view of the brick wall of the next tenement, one foot away. But it wasn't too bad a view because in the other brick wall was a window into a room where two young dames lived, and I spent some otherwise nothing evenings with my light out, watching these two broads undress.

Till one night when my landlady came in and caught me at it, and she gave me a lecture hotter than a *felsher's* poultice.

What is a *felsher?* In certain areas and times in the *shtetlach* (Jewish villages in the old country) often the only acting doctor was the *felsher*. He was a man who was essentially a barber, but he also served as a dentist and an amateur doctor. The *felsher* put cure-all poultices on you, called *bankis* (bahng-kus)—made out of plants and roots and sometimes ground-up insects—and his poultices made many people well when there was nothing else to make them well.

But the poultices he slapped on were very hot, like the lecture Grace's mother's cousin had just given me about Tom-peeping on the naked dames.

My landlady was always worried about expenses, expenses. When I'd come in late at night and go into the living room to call anybody on the phone, she'd sneak her little head into the room and say, "Mickey, I'm a poor woman—no long-distance calls, please."

Meanwhile, there was no job for me—anywhere. When I first got to New York, I deposited my card with the New York Musicians Union; but they told me that jobs were scarce, and since I was new in town, I'd have to take my chances on "the floor." This was a huge barnlike room on the second floor of the union hall, with little audition rooms around the perimeter. On Mondays, when most of what hiring there was took place, there would be as many as a thousand starving musicians milling around the floor, all carrying their instruments—even the bass and tuba players— all waiting hopefully for their names to be called, so they could make a few bucks. Actually, it was usually the instrument that was called. The bullhorn would bellow, "Trombone player wanted for Italian funeral!"

It was a hell of a letdown for the boy clarinet genius from Cleveland. At this point you could have got odds that I would never conquer New York or survive till Passover.

One of my worst experiences on the floor concerned a bandleader named—I kid you not—Sam Schmulevitz, who played weddings and bar mitzvahs on the Lower East Side. One Monday on the floor I was clutching my clarinet, hoping against hope for a job, when suddenly the bullhorn blasted, "Clarinet and sax man for a bar mitzvah! Go to Room Three!"

My heart thumping, I rushed to audition Room 3 and was introduced to Sam Schmulevitz. (It seems all the band leaders hiring anybody were either Jewish or Italian.) Sam had a rich Harvard accent. He said, "Katz, you woiking Sotaday?"

When I said that I was quite busy but I wasn't engaged for Saturday, he said, "You got a tuxedo and a black-ball tie?"

When I said "Yes," his next question was, "You play a Jewish 'clorinet'?"

I never knew that clarinets were classified by religion; what he meant was could I play the Eastern European Yiddish music. When I said, "Of course," he went on, "Can you also play a tzymbal?"

That was too much. I said, "Mr. Schmulevitz, to play a clarinet or a saxophone takes both hands. How the hell can I play a cymbal at the same time?"

He said, "It's a foot tzymbal; you play it sitting down."

I was still hot. "Mr. Schmulevitz, what will you be doing?"

Sam was cool. He said, "I play the wiolin, sitting down, and with my right foot I play the bass drum. With Hymie on the accordion, we got plenty rhythm."

The bar mitzvah that Saturday night was held at the Rivington Gardens, a huge second-floor kosher catering emporium in the center of the Lower East Side. There must have been four hundred people there. Tough little kids threw scraps of knishes and sponge cake into the bell of my saxophone, and worse, they kept kicking my foot cymbal forty feet away from me. I had to go crawling after it through the sea of legs.

Scale for the job was six bucks. When Mr. Schmulevitz paid me, after five hours of playing clarinet and sax and stomping on the goddamned cymbal, he gave be only five bucks—a dollar under the scale. I said indignantly, "I blew my brains out, and you're trying to screw me!"

He said, "Katz, to tell you the truth, you play a good clorinet, but a lousy tzymbal."

Now at this time of severe unemployment among the musicians in New York there was a place called Charlie's Tavern, at Seventh Avenue and Fifty-second Street. At noon every day there must have been five hundred unemployed musicians trying to get in. Beer was a nickel, and with a nickel beer you got a free hard-boiled egg. If you were agile, you could sneak an extra hard-boiled egg or two out of the big bowl. It was a godsend. For years many unemployed musicians "ate at Charlie's."

But after ten days of it I'd had enough already. I was going down Broadway one day, hoping to meet somebody I knew—*anybody*—when I ran into a cousin of Grace's named Lou Seltzer, who was a struggling actor. He said, "Why don't we do an act together?"

"What kind of an act?"

"We'll do a double. You play the clarinet, and I'll play the harmonica; we'll tell a few jokes, sing a few songs. . . ."

"What'll we call the act?"

"Louis & Kay."

We're not even started yet, and he wants top billing!

In those days there were probably a hundred theaters in and around New York that presented one-night "stage shows." They called them professional tryouts, but what they were was a slightly professional version of amateur night. They'd pay you $5 to $10, and if you went over big, they'd book you into a better neighborhood the next week and pay you maybe $12. If you laid a bomb, they'd yank you off the stage with the hook, or you could be knocked senseless by the hunks of garbage, bottles, and other debris thrown at you by the audience. Times Square must have had fifty agents who booked these professional tryout "acts," and out of your $5 or $10 they took 10 percent.

That's how Louis & Kay started. An agent named Jack Sterling got us an $8 booking at a theater on Tenth Avenue. The audience was as Irish as Paddy's pig, except for a sprinkling of tough Italians. Now I know why the song in the Broadway musical *"On Your Toes"* was called "Slaughter on Tenth Avenue." Lou and I bounced out and told a couple of jokes—bad ones—sang a couple of songs, badly . . . and that Irish and Italian audience started throwing everything at us but the seats. I started playing some Irish reels, and we managed, just barely, to get off alive.

We came offstage, our agent, Jack Sterling, was there; as he helped to brush the garbage off us, he said, "Boys, you're going to have to shape up your act a little."

I said, "Mr. Sterling, our act just doesn't have any shape."

I said goodbye to Louis & Kay and went walking down Broadway again. This time I was luckier. I ran into a man named Ed Fishman, who was one of the biggest band bookers in the world—literally and "figuratively." I'd met Fishman in Cleveland; he was a tremendous man who weighed about three hundred and fifty pounds; he looked like Paul Whiteman, but was twice as big. And his heart was just as big. When I told him that things were going a little tough, he said, "You come and live with me, move right in today, and I'll help you find work."

That very afternoon, as soon as I could thank Cousin Treine and get my things—and promise not to look at any more naked dames—I moved from the East Bronx to Ed Fishman's beautiful apartment on West End Avenue. It was like moving from hell to heaven, not only to be away from Tiffany Street, but to be back in the world of music. I lived with Ed for two or three weeks, till he found me a job playing clarinet and sax in Howard Phillips' orchestra at the Manger Hotel. (Hell of a place for a Jewish boy to be playing. Fortunately they pronounced it the Mang-ger, with a hard *g*. Later it became the Taft.) One of the great players in the band was trombonist Mike Riley, who later had his own band and made a tremendous hit with his song "The Music Goes 'Round and 'Round."

The important thing was that my new job paid sixty-eight cash bucks a week!

Now that I was employed, my premarital situation back in Cleveland began to heat up. Meaning that I was spending too much of my sixty-eight bucks a week on long-distance calls to Grace, to tell her how much I loved her. After a

month of this she said, "Mickey, you'd better come home
and marry me if you're going to—because I'm not going to
wait any longer." (After all, she wasn't getting any younger
—she was seventeen.)

So I wrote a long letter to my mother, telling her that I
wanted to come home and marry Grace.

When my mother got the letter, she called me collect.
She said fervently, "Mickey, *mein kind* [my child], you're
very young. Someday you will get married, and I hope you
will be very happy; but how could it hurt if you wait a
little while?" I knew that what she meant was how could it
hurt to wait maybe thirty more years. It broke my heart to
hear my mother's pleas because I knew what heartbreak it
was for her. I was not only one of her loving sons, but a big
part of her dream of security for her old age. I could only
keep saying, "Mama, I know how you feel; but I love
Grace, and I'm going to marry her."

Forty dollars later my mother accepted the inevitable. In
a sweet, defeated voice that wrung the very soul out of me,
she said, "All right, Mickey. Send me ten dollars for a new
dress, so I'll look nice for the wedding."

I went home, and Grace and I got married, to a sellout
crowd at the Euclid Avenue Temple. Grace's folks belonged
to a Reformed temple, and my folks were Orthodox, so I
was caught in the middle again. But we solved that by
having my grandfather act as cantor, chanting the marriage
benediction under the *chuppa* (wedding canopy), alongside
the Epsteins' beloved Rabbi Barnett Brickner.

After the ceremony Grace's papa and mama gave us a
beautiful wedding reception at the Jewish Center, for two
hundred and fifty people. Since Gracie was their first
daughter to get married, they went all out on the wedding
and the reception. Like all young bridegrooms with no
money, I was looking longingly at the envelopes that were
being given to us by the well-wishers. At even five bucks per
envelope, Grace and I would go back to New York
millionaires!

As soon as I could discreetly take a peek, I began sneaking looks into the envelopes. I'd forgotten that most of our friends, like me, were of very limited means. One uncle I'd really been depending on gave us $2. A note in another envelope said, "If you will go to Newman's Department Store, you will find paid for you a waffle iron."

By the time I could take a fast count I had $90, a waffle iron, and Grace.

We rushed to grab the train back to New York, where I was, thank God, still working. A big spender, I had reserved a drawing room on the train, for $42. My good friend Tony Alongi, who played sax with us at the Manger, met us at Grand Central Station in his open convertible. I rode triumphantly down Broadway with my new bride. What a wonderful feeling! I felt like the toast of New York. Then Tony whispered to me, "The hotel was raided last night—for gambling, booze, and broads," and we were out of a job!

I'd reserved the honeymoon suite at the Victoria Hotel, and since it was our honeymoon, we stayed for two days. Then, with all my money gone, we moved in with Grace's Aunt Annie in Coney Island. Five people in a tiny little flat near the beach. It wasn't the way I had intended my marriage to Gracie to start. But that's the way the kishka krumbles.

To the rescue—Grace's Uncle Louie!

Uncle Louie and his wife, Sadie, lived in North Arlington, New Jersey, a northern suburb of Newark. For fifty years Uncle Louie ran a well-known hardware store on Ridge Road, with rooms over the store. But it was a commodious apartment, and when they came over to see us at Aunt Annie's, Uncle Louie said why didn't we go to their house and stay with them. Why not indeed? We accepted.

Sadie was a great hostess and a fabulous cook of Jewish delicacies. When Grace and I would be enjoying her great *latkes* (potato pancakes), Sadie would stand proudly back of our chairs and say, "You feel it?" Boy, did we feel it!

But what I needed was a job. While we lived with

wonderful Uncle Louie and Aunt Sadie, I played a few casual dates around New York, anything I could find. This was April 1930. One of the few sources of income for one-night musicians at that time was playing in orchestras at fraternity houses at the colleges, particularly the Ivy League colleges. People occasionally ask me what college I went to. I tell them Princeton, Harvard, Yale, and Dartmouth. I got straight A's in Saturday night dixieland. One night I was playing at a fraternity dance at Princeton. During a break I wandered over to the fraternity house next door. They were having a break, too, and their bandleader was sitting on the stairs eating a chicken leg. He was Louis Armstrong.

Then I received a long-distance call from Cleveland, from Jack Spector, an old friend and a great trumpet player. Jack was playing for Maurice Spitalny at Loew's State Theater in Cleveland—and Maurice needed a clarinet and sax man. Jack had recommended me, Maurice had agreed to hire me, and the salary was $99 a week. Wowwwwwwwwwww!

I hardly waited to pack. I kissed Uncle Louie and Aunt Sadie, grabbed Grace by the hand, and we rushed for the train back to Cleveland.

You will perhaps wonder how Maurice Spitalny knew me well enough to hire me sight unseen. Actually, I didn't know Maurice Spitalny at all. But he knew me from my association with his brother Phil, who was later to become internationally famous with his All-Girl Orchestra.

The Spitalnys were one of the most amazing families in the whole American musical scene. The father, Jacob Spitalny, had come to Cleveland some thirty years before with his three musical sons—a Jewish immigrant family from a village in the Ukraine called Tetiyev. (The immigrants from this one Russian village built their own synagogue in Cleveland, on Linn Drive.)

After they settled in Cleveland, Jacob Spitalny taught piano and violin and was also an orchestra leader. For a time he and his sons played together at the Perry Theater on Woodland Avenue, where Yiddish shows were presented. Phil played the clarinet, and Maurice and the oldest son, H. Leopold Spitalny, played violin.

Then Phil became the conductor at the Allen Theater. Maurice became the conductor at Cleveland's Loew's State and Palace theaters, leaving in the 1940s to become musical director of Pittsburgh's famous pioneer radio station, KDKA. H. Leopold Spitalny left Cleveland in the early thirties and became head of NBC Music in New York. They were an absolutely amazingly talented family.

I first met Phil Spitalny in April 1927. He was then conducting the orchestra at the Allen Theater, and his brother Maurice at that early time was conducting the orchestra at the Stillman Theater.

While at the Allen, Phil developed all his symphonic presentations, à la Paul Whiteman, but with a much smaller band. He had a very talented pianist, assistant conductor, and arranger named Jerry Mayhall. Jerry, who had been a fine conductor, called me up at home one day and asked me to come down to the Allen Theater between shows and audition for Phil. I was seventeen and just out of high school. But Jerry and Phil had heard of my clarinet and sax work. Jerry said that Phil was about to leave on an eastern tour and was looking for a good clarinet and sax man, someone who among other things could play the clarinet introduction to *Rhapsody in Blue.* This is a difficult passage, but I could play it.

I took my clarinet and alto sax and went down to the Allen Theater. In the theater's music library Jerry was sitting at the piano, and Phil Spitalny was pacing up and down, resplendent in his silk robe and Vaseline pompadour. He said, "All right, kid, let's hear somethin'."

Jerry at the piano gave me the opening chord of *Rhapsody in Blue,* and I played that famous opening glissando clarinet cadenza. When I finished, Phil said, "You play good clarinet, kid. Let's hear the saxophone." I proceeded to play my alto sax, sight-reading one of his overtures.

After a half hour Phil stopped the audition and said, "You help support your mother and father?"

I said, "Yes, of course I do."

He said, "Well I'm going to pay you eighty-five dollars a week, and you're going on the road tour with us! You're a nice kid."

I rehearsed with the Phil Spitalny band for a week at the Allen Theater, and in early May we left for Boston from the East Fifty-fifth and Euclid Penn Station. My family and a lot of friends were there to see me off, my family as tearful as though I were leaving for Tibet.

And there in that crowd at the railroad station was where I first saw beautiful little dark-eyed Grace Epstein. She was fourteen and the most beautiful thing I'd ever seen in my life. How she happened to be there at all was a sheer coincidence. My brother, Al, had been with a group of young people at the Euclid Avenue Temple, where Grace was being confirmed. When he said that he was going to the railroad station to see me off to Boston, she said sure, she'd like to come along and wave goodbye to Mickey Katz. That was fifty years ago, and we haven't waved goodbye to each other yet. I started writing to her on the train and wrote her every day from Boston. As soon as I could get back to Cleveland, we started dating, and neither one of us ever dated anyone else.

Boston is not known as Fun City, but it was for me in 1927—a seventeen-year-old boy on his first trip away from home. I was a scared, unsophisticated little Jewish kid; I'd never eaten milk and meat together. Our first night in Boston some of the other members of the orchestra took me to an Italian restaurant called Stella's, where I had a lot of red wine and passed out colder than a kosher clam. (In 1966 I was performing in Boston in *Hello, Solly,* and just for nostalgia, thirty-nine years later, I took Grace over to Stella's. It was still there, and so was Stella, or at least the same elderly lady who was the proprietor on my fateful night. I asked her if she remembered anything about a night many years ago when the Phil Spitalny orchestra was in there. "Oh, yes," she said, remembering. "You must be the leetla boy who gotta sick.")

While we were playing Loew's State in Boston, there was another show in town at the Colonial Theater called *Twinkle Twinkle*. With a title like that, you knew that it had to have a lot of pretty girls.

Well, almost immediately there was a hotel employees' strike, which closed all the big commercial hotels in Boston, including the one where the *Twinkle Twinkle* girls were staying. As it happened, we were staying at a little Back Bay hotel, the Astor, which was across the street from the Christian Science mother church. Our little hotel wasn't struck. But when the chorus line of *Twinkle Twinkle* came over to see about rooms, there weren't any. Then Eddie Inski, our Polish tuba player, had a brilliant idea. He said, "Girls, I'll tell you what we'll do: We'll *share* our rooms with you!" Which we did, and during the next couple of weeks there were times when my back ached so much I could hardly make it to the theater.

Actually, the Phil Spitalny musical performances onstage were magnificent, if I do say so. Phil had only ten men in his road band, but they all were terrific musicians. He had a sensational saxophone player named Stubby Gordon, whose beautiful sound I have never heard duplicated.

And Jerry Mayhall arranged symphonic effects for Phil's ten men that you wouldn't believe. We played the *1812 Overture,* complete with cannon! For the cannon sounds, we had stagehands fire blank shotguns into empty barrels. It would reverberate through the theater; you'd swear it was artillery.

It worked great till one of the stagehands got drunk. When it came cannon time, instead of firing his blank shotgun into the barrel, he fired straight into the curtain and set the curtain on fire. Spitalny took one look at the flames and yelled, "For God's sake, get de vater hose! Vater, vater! Either vater or let down de curtain!"

In that era, 1927, any stage or dance bandleader was always besieged by song pluggers. Radio was really just getting started; there were no sound movies and no television. The only way the song publishers could plug their new songs was to hire guys to do a persistent sell job on their new songs with the orchestra leaders around the country.

While we were in Boston, there was an indefatigable song plugger named Charlie Goldberg who was always vainly trying to see Phil at the theater. He'd come in almost every day and ask to see Spitalny, but Phil wouldn't see him. He had no interest in seeing him. One day Goldberg asked Stubby Gordon what nationality Spitalny was. Stubby, who had a gagman's love of comic situations, told him that Spitalny was a descendant of a fine old Italian family with aristocratic forebears. Goldberg thanked him profusely for this "information."

Phil used to wear silk BVDs with the flap in the back. Before going onstage, he'd take a little walk around backstage in his silk drawers to air out his parts.

Well, one day when Phil came strolling out of his dressing room in his silk BVDs, Charlie-on-the-spot Goldberg was there to greet him. Charlie stepped up and in his most courtly manner bowed and said, "Signor Spitalny, *buon giorno!*"

Phil looked at him and said, "And who de fuck are you?"

Phil had trouble saying his Vs; they came out Wees. I'll never forget our first rehearsal on "Varsity Drag," the new hit of the day. Phil said, "Today we're going to act like college boys. I've got de hats for you [little beanies], and we're going to sing a new number. You spell it Wee-a-r-s-i-t-y, Warsity Drag."

That's the way we rehearsed it, and that's the way we sang it in the first show—"Warsity Drag." The manager of the theater almost committed suicide.

Phil Spitalny was one of the greatest technicians on the clarinet that I've ever heard. He was also a colorful and kindly man. Years after I'd left him—so I could stay in Cleveland with Grace—Phil was always inquiring about me, asking how I was getting along.

Incidentally, don't believe all that stuff you've heard about his later All-Girl Orchestra being men musicians in falsies. He had very talented girl musicians and entertainers. In fact, he divorced his wife and married his All-Girl solo violinist. Remember "Evelyn and Her Magic Violin"? She and Phil were married for nearly forty years, till Phil's death just a few years ago.

Believe me, I knew the Spitalnys. And Maurice Spitalny knew enough about my clarinet and sax playing to hire me sight unseen.

With my new ninety-nine bucks a week playing for Maurice, I took an apartment for Grace and me on Overlook Road in Cleveland Heights, one of the nicest parts of town. I've always liked to go first class if I thought I could make it.

When we moved into Overlook Road, we didn't know it at the time, but we were preparing a nest to welcome Joel.

With the wonderful new job and the lovely new apartment, Grace completed our joy a year later by announcing that she was pregnant. Our delight gradually changed to concern as she sailed blithely past the nine months with no sign of giving birth. When she was well past the normal term, she felt *something,* so I rushed her to Mount Sinai Hospital. She called early the next morning and said brightly, "Hello, dear, come and get me."

I said, "Is the baby born?"

She said, "No, false alarm."

So I brought her home. Some ten days later, when she was now *way* past the nine months her doctor decided to take her back to the hospital and try to induce labor. (That's always sounded to me as if mothers should have a union.)

So they induced labor pains. I was busy working at Loew's State because we were going to need all the money we could get for the baby. But finally, Grace had been at the hospital for six or eight hours, and nothing much was happening.

Forlorn and disheartened, I knew that things were not going well. So now I did take off from work, and Grace's mother and I sat around the hospital, waiting for some good news—which wasn't forthcoming.

After a while I took Grace's mother out to get her some dinner, and not knowing anything else to do, we stopped by the nice apartment on Overlook Road to make sure that everything was ready for "the baby" in the beautiful new nursery Grace had got all ready.

Then Grace's mother and I got a call from the hospital that we'd better get back over there. When we got there, things were rapidly going from bad to worse. Grace had been in labor for some sixteen hours, and nothing was going right. Finally, Dr. Abrams—he was one of the best obstetricians in Cleveland—came out of the delivery room and talked to us. He said that the baby's head was just not moving, and in a situation like this—he used the words "God forbid"—the doctors sometimes had to decide whether to save the baby or the mother. They wouldn't know anything definite for a while, so it might be better for us to go take a little ride, get some air. My mother-in-law and I drove back over to the apartment and sat there, looking at the new nursery and crying, for a couple of hours. We hadn't heard anything more, but we finally went back over to the hospital.

By now my mother and father were there. We sat around silently as the minutes, and our lives, ticked away. It got to be two o'clock in the morning. Maybe it was three. The clocks all seemed to have stopped. The whole world seemed to have stopped.

Then suddenly one of the nurses came running out to us. She said that the doctors were one moment away from sacrificing the baby to save Grace when suddenly the baby's head had started to move! Just a little, but things might still be all right. Please, God.

And, finally, they were. Joel arrived in this world with some historic forceps marks on his head, but he arrived in one piece.

Not knowing any other way to give thanks, I went rushing out to Solomon's all-night delicatessen and came back with two big sacks of corned beef sandwiches for the doctors and the nurses in the maternity ward of Mount Sinai.

After Grace and Joel had been home for a week or so, I started proudly bringing people in to see him. I thought he was beautiful. He didn't have a hair on his head, his head was tremendously big for the rest of him—he weighed seven pounds eleven ounces when he was born, mostly head —and he still bore the forceps marks that made him look as if he'd been through the Battle of the Bulge. He had.

In our apartment house lived a great trombone player, Al Angelotta, who played with me at Loew's State. One night when we came home from the theater after the show, I brought Al in to see Joel. On the way into our apartment I said, "You've never seen such a beautiful baby in your whole life."

Al took a long look at baldheaded little Joel. Then he said, "That your kid? . . . Good luck, Katz."

This is me, at age five, the family bugler.

Mama and Papa, 1905.

Sister Estelle, aged ten, a veteran
of amateur nights.

My first tuxedo and wing
collar. At fourteen, I'm
posing for the first time as
a pro.

My Mama costumed for the role of Yeckele the Innkeeper.

My beloved zayde (grandpa), the family anchor of love.

My darling wife Grace, age fifteen. Still the girl of my dreams.

Me on the right, age sixteen, playing saxophone in Cleveland's Fenway Hall Hotel orchestra.

My first big band—1929.

Papa, Mama and me aboard the steamer **Goodtime**.

Married but not worried—1930.

(Above) *First portrait—Grace and baby Joel.*
(Below, left) *Portrait of son Ronnie, at age
one.* (Below, right) *Joel, wearing his new coat,
made by his grandfather with loving hands.*

Family portrait—1938.

Early recording session—Capitol Records. From the left, front row, Joel, A & R man Lou Bush, violinist Benny Gill, trombonist Si Zentner, a special guitarist for the session, arranger-pianist Nat Farber, Mannie Klein, myself. Rear, left, bassist Larry Breen, right, drummer Sammy Weiss. (Rothschild Photo)

Onstage at the mike with Spike.

Chorus line—Borscht Capades, *New York, 1950.* (Talbot-Giles)

Album cover, Mickey Katz Plays Music for Weddings, Bar Mitzvahs and Brisses, *1951.* (Courtesy Capitol Records, Inc.)

(Right) *Album cover,* "Mish-Mosh," *Capitol Records, 1950.* (Courtesy Capitol Records, Inc.)

Backstage at the Blackstone Theater, Chicago, 1950—me and Menasha Skulnik, the famous clown prince of the Yiddish theater. (Alexander Spivak)

Joel making like Eddie Cantor, after signing for the Colgate Comedy Hour.

At New Frontier in Las Vegas, 1954. Was I in good company!

Grace and I arriving in London, 1956. (Matthews' News and Photo Agency)

*Ronnie saying "I do."
Maddie saying "Me
too." 1956.* (Arnhoelter-
Thompson Photog-
raphy)

*In 1958 came another
great day when Jo
Wilder became Mrs.
Joel Grey.*

Grace and "Dopey" Klein, Mannie's wife, strike up the band at the Sydney, Australia, airport.

Airport at Capetown, South Africa, 1961. A thrilling welcome by the "Cape Coloureds" band and chorus. (Cape Times Photograph)

My creative wife at her Grace Gallery at I. Magnin's in Beverly Hills.

Grace and I guesting on the Mike Douglas Show *with co-host Joel, 1973.*

A recent picture of His Worship the Mayor of Capetown, and his wife, our 1961 southern Africa tour hosts.

With George Jessel, toastmaster of the United States, presiding at my 50th-Anniversary-In-Show-Business roast at the Beverly Hills Club, 1975.
(Irv Antter)

Grace and I with daughter-in-law Jo Grey and grandson Jimmy at Fairmont Hotel in San Francisco in 1976, during Joel's engagement there.

My fabulous mother-in-law, Grandma Fanny, sitting in our living room enjoying her daughter's artistry.

My grandchildren Jennifer and Jimmy Grey.

Grandson Todd Katz's bar mitzvah, 1975. Left to right, Grandpa Mickey, Grandma "Dacie," Todd, Great-Grandmother Fanny, daughter-in-law Maddie, son Ron, grandson Randy.

Grace and I greeting Menachem Begin, hero of Israel's War of Independence and now Prime Minister, at a Beverly Hills rally for Israel.

4 · The Steamer Goodtime Shook, Rattled and Rolled

I WORKED FOR MAURICE SPITALNY at Cleveland's Loew's State Theater during 1930, '31, and '32. Then Maurice moved over to conduct the orchestra at the RKO Palace Theater. I stayed on at Loew's State for another year, playing under the new leader, violinist Myron Roman. Then around 1933 I rejoined Maurice, at the Palace, and played for him for two more years.

The two theaters presented completely different types of stage shows. Loew's State was a presentation house. The stage shows were called Loew's Units—they were produced at the Capitol Theater in New York; then they toured the Loew's theaters in Washington, Pittsburgh, Cleveland, Detroit, Chicago, and other cities. The masters of ceremonies included such luminaries as Dick Powel, who was to become a big movie star, and Paul Ash, who had gained great fame with his orchestra at the Oriental Theater in Chicago. Also, the Loew's State Unit shows all featured a chorus line of talented girls called the Chester Hale Dancers.

The Loew's State productions were great pieces of entertainment. One of the first that I remember playing was the Benny Davis Revue—a show of talented teenagers who included Martha Raye, dancer Hal Leroy, Vilma and Buddy Ebsen (at that time Buddy and his sister had a dance act), and singer Little Jackie Heller. And, of course, there was songwriter Benny Davis, acting as MC and singing his hit songs, among them being "Margie." Davis, incidentally, had a funny quirk; he carried his own cymbal with him because it had a certain "ring" that he liked. He handed it reverently to the local drummer in each theater where his revue played. Between the ring and the ping he drove the local drummers crazy.

The Loew's State shows, in addition to the big stage presentations, included a concert on the mighty organ, first-run movies, and a newsreel.

And do you know what a ticket cost? If you came to the early show, the admission was twenty-five cents! The movie would come on at eleven; as the movie finished, the orchestra musicians would drift into the pit, to play the overture and on through the newsreel and the trailers of coming attractions. Then came the big stage show. After the stage show the feature would come back on, and the whole thing would start over again. Five times daily. For your early-show twenty-five cents, you could stay from eleven in the morning till eleven at night, if you had the time and a strong sitter. Some of the Loew's State stage shows of that era traveled with three or four baggage cars of scenery and stage effects and a cast of fifty or sixty people.

The RKO Palace was a "vaudeville and picture house," but the home of major vaudeville like the Palace in New York. The shows at our Palace also included first-run movies and newsreels, while the stage shows consisted of a famous headliner and five or six supporting acts. There was no MC; the acts were "introduced," as at every vaudeville house in the country, by electrically operated annunciator cards. This was a device at the side of the stage which held big oblong name cards; as each act finished, the next card would flip down with the name of the succeeding act.

While I played for Maurice Spitalny at the Cleveland Palace, the headliners included the Ritz Brothers, Irene Bordoni, Edith Piaf, Sophie Tucker, Burns & Allen, Jack

Benny, and Milton Berle with his mother sitting in the upper box, acting as his stooge. And what was the admission? To the early show, twenty-five cents!

This even included Ethel Barrymore. I'll never forget her. We had a baldheaded fiddler in the orchestra, and one day right in the middle of a show Ethel pointed at him and yelled, "Get that man out of there! He keeps scratching his bald head—AND HE'S DRIVING ME CRAZY!" The poor guy was excused with pay and didn't reappear till Ethel had left town.

A more delightful personality who appeared at the Palace was movie siren Jean Harlow. Her straight man was NTG (Nils T. Granulund), who in the early days was an actor, as well as a producer of stage and screen musicals. He told our theater manager he needed a little guy to do a comic bit with Jean. Even then I did comedy bits, so I was tapped for the spot. Harlow paid the $100 for a substitute to take my place in the pit for the week.

I was Jean Harlow's Jewish lover for thirty-five glorious shows.

This was the bit:

There was a scene in which Harlow was relaxing in sexy lounging pajamas in her boudoir, with a big clothes wardrobe with doors at one side of the set. NTG would enter, the tired husband home from the office. He'd take her in his arms, give her a big phony kiss, and say, "Oh, my darling, I've missed you so. What have you been doing all day?" She'd answer, "Just waiting for you, my precious."

At which point the drummer in the pit would make a loud scratching noise. NTG would look up and say, "What's that noise? Have you been having trouble with mice?" Then he'd look over at the wardrobe and add, "I think I smell a rat."

As he came over to investigate, I'd throw open the doors of the big wardrobe closet and be standing there, wearing long underwear and a derby hat, holding my clarinet. I'd say, "Who's a rrrrrrrrrrat?" It always got a big laugh. After the closing performance Jean Harlow gave me a $25 bonus and a bottle of pefume for Grace.

When I say that Harlow wore sexy lounging pajamas, I am not kidding. They were high-cut, but *thin,* a real peekaboo. Many of the sexy stars in those days wore some very revealing costumes onstage. They proved highly exciting to some of our male customers. Hot flushes—hoo-ha!

I'll never forget one of our customers during the run of the *Folies Bergère.* The French dancers were scantily clad, with the star hardly clad at all, and almost every day, when the theater opened, a big swarthy man about sixty, with a Never-on-Sunday mustache, would come in and take a seat in the front row. We noticed him particularly because although it was June, he always wore an overcoat. During the show he'd watch the sexy French star onstage like a cat watching an uncaged canary. When she started her gyrations, a heat wave came over him. We'd see his hand slip down under the overcoat, and we'd say, "Oh-oh, there he goes!" Sure enough, suddenly his eyes would pop out, and our piano player would say,"The bird just flew." Next day there he'd be again.

And it wasn't only the men. Maurice Spitalny was tall and handsomely built, and when he was conducting, he'd wear a pair of tight white flannel pants that showed off his "figure." In the overture he'd always play a solo—such as "When a Gypsy Makes His Violin Cry"—and when he'd slur the notes Gypsy-style and pose with his concealed but well-endowed parts stuck out a bit, ladies in the first few rows would slump down in their seats and go, "Ohhhhhhhhhhhhhhh . . ." like bobby soxers at a 1940 Sinatra concert.

One of my other favorite acts at the Palace, though for a different reason, was my talented friends the Ritz Brothers —Harry, Al, and Jimmy. Only Harry and Jimmy are left, living in, thank goodness, healthy retirement in Las Vegas. Harry Ritz is one of the funniest men in the history of show business.

I always liked to hang out with the actors. One night after the last show, Harry Ritz said, "Katz, where can I get a good corned beef sandwich?"

I said, "Harry, come with me."

We got into my Willys-Knight and drove up to One Hundred and Fifth Street and Massie Avenue, which was the center of the Jewish community. We went into Solomon's Delicatessen. Harry told the waiter that he'd like a corned beef sandwich on rye bread, but before his sandwich he'd like some lox and cream cheese on a bagel.

The waiter said, "A corned beef sandwich on rye bread I can give you, but I don't got it any bagels till one o'clock." Meaning that at one o'clock the fresh hot bagels would be ready in the little bakery next door, and as they had done for thirty years, a waiter would go over and get some for Solomon's. During the bagel baking the bakery was not "open," but in hot weather the bakers kept the front door open at night to keep the place cool. Nobody ever robbed anybody in those days.

Well, Harry Ritz had no intention of waiting till one o'clock for a bagel—not with a bagel bakery next door. He marched over there, opened the screen door, went in, and started banging on the counter. The old baker came out from the back room, wiping his hands on his apron, and said, "Don't make so much noise. What's it all about it?"

Harry said, "We want some bagels."

The old man said, "Bagels you can have at one o'clock."

Harry, who liked to put on everybody, said, "I want some bagels right now, or I'm going back there and wreck your *farkockte* bagel machine."

Well, Harry Ritz is a big muscular guy. The little baker looked at him, then called into the back room, "Sam, bring out six bagels."

The assistant in the back room said, "It's not one o'clock yet."

The owner, with another look at Harry, said, "Sam, don't

be a shmuck. I know it's not one o'clock yet, but bring out six bagels. Immediately."

The assistant brought out six bagels in a sack, nice and hot, and Harry said, "How much?"

The old baker said, "Nothing. Just get the hell out and don't bodder me anymore." Harry tossed a dollar on the counter, and we went back over to Solomon's.

Not telling the waiter what we had in the sack, Harry said he'd like some lox and cream cheese on a bagel. The gruff old flatfooted waiter said, "I told you the bagels don't come out till one o'clock."

Harry handed him the sack. "Here's six. Have one with us."

After that Harry had two corned beef sandwiches and two glasses of chocolate soda water, which in those days in Cleveland we called Jew beers. They were the Middle West equivalent of a New York City egg cream.

Now let's set down the facts of the musicians' strike as I remember them, the strike which triggered the end of theater employment for musicians all over the country.

The musicians' strike in Cleveland concerned only the musicians in the variety theaters, which was, of course, only part of the employed musicians. Cleveland has always been a great center of musical activity. Starting at the top, we had the Cleveland Symphony, which today is one of the world's finest.

In addition to the symphony, which provided employment for more than a hundred musicians, we had the lovely Hanna Theater, which presented Broadway stage plays and musicals. We also had the big variety and vaudeville theaters—not only Loew's State and the Palace and the Hippodrome, but great suburban theaters, including the RKO 105th Street, where I first saw Bob Hope onstage. These theaters seated anywhere from twenty-five hundred to four thousand; the Hippodrome even presented *Jumbo*, complete with elephants, and very busy stagehands.

Also, Cleveland had lots of nightclubs and cafés that employed musicians. During Prohibition the mob ran a lot of liquor across Lake Erie from Canada, and mobsters have always liked nightclubs as ideal hideaways for booze and broads.

But even for the mob, the broads were by no means a sure thing.

One time I was playing at a club in downtown Cleveland where the acts included a pair of beautiful girls who were acrobats. Maybe it was the nature of their work that excited the mobster owner of the nightclub. At any rate, he got the hots for one of them. But he couldn't make a score. Frustrated, he got loaded one night and tried to get the girl acrobat into his office. She wasn't an acrobat for nothing. She easily evaded him, and in a loud and clear voice—which I heard—she told him, "I work for you, but there is no fucking option in my contract."

There was yet another part of the musical picture, one that brought many of the nation's top bands to Cleveland. Radio was becoming important to the nightclubs and hotels as a means of publicity, and Cleveland was one of the few cities where the local Musicians Union permitted orchestras to broadcast on a national hookup without additional payment to the players. The Musicians Union in New York and Chicago and a lot of other cities made the bandleaders pay their men an extra $3 to $5 per broadcast. We had no such rule. So a lot of the famous bandleaders enjoyed playing in Cleveland because it made a lot of difference on the money they made. If a bandleader had ten men in his band and a network radio hookup six nights a week, it made a difference of maybe two hundred bucks a week out of his pocket.

So an unusual number of the top bands played in Cleveland in the early days. We had Guy Lombardo and the Royal Canadians at the Music Box, Kay Kyser and his Kollege of Musical Knowledge at the Bamboo Gardens, at the Cabin Club, Swing and Sway with Sammy Kaye . . .

plus Roll and Rock with Bert Block, and Shake Your Ass with Mickey Katz.

But what caused the Cleveland musicians' strike in the mid-thirties was none of this. The strike was aggravated by the big touring stage bands that had started coming through town and playing at the Cleveland theaters—Benny Goodman, Duke Ellington, Tommy Dorsey, Woody Herman, Count Basie, and Chick Webb with a cute new girl singer named Ella Fitzgerald.

When these big stage bands hit town, the pit musicians were members of the same Musicians Union as those guys sitting up there tooting on the stage, but we'd sit in the pit and get paid for doing nothing. With Depression business bad in the theaters, this naturally became a big bone of contention between the theater owners and the union. The theater owners said why the hell should they pay two bands and have the pit orchestra sit on their collective *tochis*. The union said because you've got a contract with us—and you have to pay us.

Before the strike this situation was resolved to some extent. The theater owners and the union made a deal that when there was a touring band onstage, the theater would pay the pit orchestra 75 percent of its salary and the men wouldn't even have to show up. This was pretty sweet. I was making $100 a week. I could now draw $75 the week I didn't work and just loaf. With the theaters struggling for customers we might have stage bands five weeks in a row. Benny Goodman, Tommy Dorsey. . . . I'd put the family in the car and go to Florida. Sometimes the theaters would even give you an advance on your salary if you needed it for the trip!

But finally the big theater chains, especially Loew's and RKO, got tired of this. They told the Cleveland Musicians Union that they wanted this free ride for the pit orchestra out—period. Furthermore, since Depression business was so bad and the Cleveland theater musicians were all making a good salary, they wanted us to take a ten percent cut.

Instead of which the Cleveland union called us out on strike.

We thought the theaters could never do without us. The president of our local union at that time was Otto Kapl. I remember one strike meeting we held in the parking lot of the Palace Theater. Otto was telling us about Mr. Addison, who was the representative of the theater owners. Otto said, "Now, when Mr. Addison tells you that you have to take a cut in salary, you say, 'Yes sir, Mr. Addison. . . . Yes sir, Mr. Addison. . . . Get lost, Mr. Addison.' "

Well, the finish was that *we* got lost. Mr. Addison won the war. Part of it was the fact that Hollywood was now making big musicals in sound and Technicolor. The stage show was now on the screen—the singers, the dancers, the musicians, everybody. The theaters didn't need musicians in the pit anymore because there was nobody on the stage anymore.

The musicians didn't realize what was happening. We'd played in theaters for so many years that to us it was a sure thing, a job for life. The theater owners would have to settle with us eventually; they always had. So we continued to act high and mighty; we waved our instruments in the face of a dead horse.

And finally we had to realize that not only had we lost a strike, but the whole era of employment for musicians in the theaters was bye, bye, baby. Today there is *one* theater with a permanent house orchestra—Radio City Music Hall. It employs a hundred musicians. As for the other once-thousands of variety-theater musicians all over the country, it was over, finished, dead, period, and out. Ninety percent of the variety-theater musicians never played anywhere again. Many of them were not trained or equipped to play other music; they became waiters, barbers, taxi drivers. . . .

As for me, I got lucky. My next musical stop was the lake boats. Every summer for the next five years I led my own orchestra on the excursion boats sailing out of Cleveland, and I wouldn't have missed it.

Since Cleveland was a strategically situated port on Lake Erie, boats of all kinds were very important in the life of the city. The docks at the East Ninth Street Pier were busy night and day. There was the overnight passenger boat to Buffalo, the overnight boat to Detroit, plus the freighters full of steel and other commercial products going back and forth on Lake Erie to all sorts of places.

But my world was the excursion boats. There was the *See-and-Bee,* named for the Cleveland & Buffalo Transportation Company. The *See-and-Bee* carried eight hundred passengers on a week's cruise, clear up to Sault ("Sue") Ste. Marie in Michigan, where the locks separate Lake Huron from Lake Superior. On the way up and back the *See-and-Bee* would stop at various places, including Buffalo, Chicago, the Sault and the fabulous resort of Mackinac (we called it Mackinaw) Island. After the debacle in the theaters Maurice Spitalny led the five-piece orchestra on the *See-and-Bee.*

My boat was the steamer *Goodtime*—also owned by the Cleveland & Buffalo Transportation Company—a huge old side-wheeler built in 1898 that carried as many as twenty-five hundred plucky picnickers. We didn't go as far as the *See-and-Bee,* but we steamed around Lake Erie every day. In fact, every day and every night, because when we got back from the long daytime excursion, we took another thousand adventurers out at night for the "moonlight ride."

Again, what did all this cost? The whole day's round-trip cruise over to Cedar Point—a beautiful picnic resort some sixty miles west of Cleveland—cost $1.10 ($1.35 on Sundays and holidays), with twenty-five cents extra for the added round trip during the day up to Put-in-Bay. Children were half price. After we got home from the day's excursion, the shorter moonlight ride cost sixty cents. Both these prices, as all the ads stated in big letters, included "Dancing to the music of Mickey Katz, King of Clarinetists, and his Good-time Kittens."

I am proud to say that by this time I was always featured in the publicity of whatever musical activity I was engaged in. I treasure an ad from the Hilliard Square Theater at Hilliard Road and Madison Avenue, near the exclusive Lakewood area. (This was a split-week show I played during the winter.) The ad announced: "MICKEY KATZ AND HIS ORCHESTRA, Plus a 10 People Stage Revue, every Sunday, Monday and Tuesday. Due to the great cost of this high type entertainment it will be necessary to raise our adult admission price from twenty-five cents to thirty cents on Sunday, Monday and Tuesday. . . ." That really wasn't too high a price to pay, considering that in addition to the fantastic Mickey Katz stage show, you were regaled with first-run movies.

We gave people a comparable bargain on the steamer *Goodtime*. Every morning at eight-thirty I'd have my band out on the upper deck, playing "Anchors Aweigh," as the two thousand or more people stampeded aboard with their picnic baskets. Since we knew how important the day was to these people—many of them had planned all year for this one-day's outing—we gave them the whole ceremony: the band playing out on deck, the passengers throwing colorful paper streamers, people kissing each other, such farewells!

It was a fun day for the passengers, but a long working day for us.

As soon as the boat sailed at nine, we'd go down one deck to the bandstand and play "dancing" till twelve. These people had only one day to do it all, so believe me they started dancing at nine in the morning and kept it up till twelve. Fox-trots, polkas, mazurkas, Viennese waltzes. . . .

By noon the boat would have steamed the sixty miles west to Cedar Point, with its swimming beaches and picnic grounds of all sorts. If we had two thousand people aboard, nineteen hundred would get off at Cedar Point, some with luggage to check in at the Breakers Hotel and stay several days.

After the mass unloading—at about twelve-thirty—the other hundred passengers would stay aboard and pay the extra two bits for the added round-trip up to Put-in-Bay. The musicians all had "staterooms"—little cubicles up on the top deck—and on the way up to Put-in-Bay we'd take naps.

Put-in-Bay was a smaller version of Mackinac Island. We'd get there about one-thirty. Everybody would stroll around the town, maybe buy some of the famous Catawba wines available there, and with the orchestra's "kitty" I'd buy some decent food that the boat's chef would cook for us for lunch when we got back aboard (the normal crew food aboard was more like crow food). Three o'clock—off again back to Cedar Point. The orchestra would have lunch on the way, then the boat would pick up our passengers at Cedar Point, and by four we were back on the bandstand playing for more dancing.

Adding to the activity on the *Goodtime* was the fact that as soon as we got out beyond the three-mile limit, the covers came off the slot machines. And from then on it was a spirited race between the children on board and the slot-machine manager. The kids weren't supposed to gamble. As soon as the slot-machine man would go around a corner, some kid would yell, "He's gone!" and they'd all rush to throw in a nickel before he could get back.

At four-thirty—again at sea—we put on a show! It was a good show. In addition to my band, we had a professional MC, Arthur Hartley, a couple of good vaudeville acts, and even a line of girls, the Dorothy Frank Dancers.

After the show we'd play for still more dancing, till about six-thirty, when we got back to Cleveland.

Our daytime passengers would disembark, tired but happy, but our day wasn't done. Waiting on the dock would be at least a thousand people ready for the "Moonlight

Cruise." By eight we were under way again. During the evening, as moonlit Lake Erie swept by, we played for more dancing, put on another show, and played for a lot more dancing. We finally got back into Cleveland, through for the day, around eleven-thirty. And the next morning at eight-thirty we had to be back aboard and out on deck playing "Anchors Aweigh."

Seven days a week.

How did we stand it? Well, we all were young, and it lasted only for ten weeks each summer. Also, it was big money. As the leader, I got $160 a week, and my men got $89, which in those Depression days was a fortune.

We went out in good weather and bad. I remember countless stormy days when I stood belowdecks looking down into the engine room, watching those sweaty, grimy guys hurling more and more coal into the straining boilers, and I'd wonder seriously when the boat would blow up. Our chief engineer was a huge man, about six-six, a colossus in those days. When any of his coal heavers would come aboard drunk, try to shovel coal into the boilers, and fall down, he'd pick those big guys up by their collars and beat the hell out of them. He was a tough guy, but he kept the steam up.

In all the five summers I spent on the *Goodtime* I can remember only one day when the weather was so bad that we didn't go out. There's a saying that the Great Lakes have "eleven months of bad weather—and August." Some of the weather was really foul. I remember one stormy trip when the *Goodtime* was bouncing all over Lake Erie. A big Polish gentleman came lurching over to the bandstand, sea-sick and drunk, and he said, "Hey, orchestra, play a polka." Before I could even start a polka, he puked right into my saxophone. I still think about it every time I take that horn out of the case.

The day that kept us in port the weather was even worse than that. It was a terribly cold, windy day—in late June!— and a heavy fog had rolled in. An Eskimo would have stayed in his igloo. But there were maybe fifty or sixty brave souls on the dock, waiting to go. Phil Swartz, the head of the company, came over, and for the first time in five years our Captain Spurrier said, "Phil, I don't think we ought to go out today." What he meant was that there was no way we *could* go out today unless we called the Alaska Coast Guard to borrow an icebreaker.

It seemed to be fate that whenever a Jewish organization would charter all or part of the *Goodtime,* the weather would turn from sunny to stormy. My mother, rest her soul, went along on some of these bad-weather trips, and she'd just sit in a deck chair and hardly make a move. I suppose she was praying that we should all live and be well.

Grace's mother, on the other hand, didn't give a damn about the weather. My mother-in-law, Fanny Epstein, would have been unconcerned on the *Titanic*—if she'd had a deck of cards and a few cronies. I remember one trip when she came aboard with the Jewish Center group, numbering some nine hundred. I stood on deck, playing "Anchors Aweigh," as they came aboard, and I could *smell* bad weather. I knew that the day was going to be a bummer. From the upper deck, where we were playing, I could see the waves coming over the breakwater, half a mile away from the dock.

But my mother-in-law is a strong lady. I knew that trying to advise her not to go would have had about as much effect as telling a tornado not to touch down in Topeka. I did the next best thing I could think of. I had a table set up amidships, where she and her five lady buddies could play poker.

When the tugs pulled us away from the dock, the trip started off smoothly because we were still inside the break-water. Fanny and her ladies started playing poker about nine-thirty. I heard my mother-in-law take charge of her group by saying, "Well, here we are, girls, the six of us, and I thought we'd start with a little stud poker." The others, knowing Grace's mother, said, "Certainly, Mrs. Epstein."

Then we got out past the breakwater, and the boat started to roll and toss. The dancers on the floor started spending more and more of their time *on* the floor. Little by little I saw people leaving to go look for places where they could throw up. My mother-in-law's poker players—evidently not wishing to rock *her* boat—stuck it out better than most. But finally, one of them got up and said, "Mrs. Epstein, excuse me. There's a cold in de vind, so I think I will go lie down."

She left; my mother-in-law watched her go and then said, "Ladies, with only five hands, I think we better play draw poker."

The others said, "Certainly, Mrs. Epstein."

But then another of her players excused herself and left. Fanny looked over at me as though the weather were my fault. Looking at her vanishing poker game, she said, "Ladies, with only four of us, we're going to play a little racehorse rummy."

Those remaining said, "Certainly, Mrs. Epstein."

But the weather was getting steadily worse. The next time I got a break and could walk past their table, my mother-in-law was sitting there alone, playing solitaire. She looked up from her cards and said, "You know where you can put this goddamned boat."

But in truth, most of the time the weather was beautiful, and everybody aboard had what he or she expected—a picnic. And on many of these nice days I'd take my papa and mama for a cruise. I'd get my father a little sailor hat and get my mother a little lady's sailor hat, and they loved it. During the dancing and the show my mother would walk around and say quietly to the other ladies, "The orchestra leader, he's my son."

On days like that the boat was indeed the steamer *Goodtime.*

5 · What Did You Do in the War, Daddy?

FROM THE MID-THIRTIES ON—after the strike finished employment in the theaters—I had an interesting variety of musical jobs. Playing on the boats took care of my summers into 1939, but in the winters I joined the other musicians in searching for crumbs in the snow. I took out jazz bands on icy roads on some of history's most perilous one-night stands.

Maurice Spitalny also organized a dance band, and I played for him part of the time on one-night stands. I remember one night when we were coming home on a lonely road near East Liverpool, Ohio, after a date in Pittsburgh. We were traveling in a decrepit old bus, and suddenly the muffler blew out and the bus started filling with fumes. Maurice yelled, "Open a window—I'm getting sophisticated!"

Around 1939 the steamer *Goodtime* went out of business because of increased costs and decreased patronage, so it became necessary for me to look for a new steady berth. And I got lucky: I was hired as bandleader and MC at a suburban Cleveland gambling palace called the Ohio Villa.

This was by no means my first experience playing for the gentlemen I later began to describe as the Kosher Nostra. In 1928, when I was eighteen, I had a job with my band at a nightclub called Shore Acres, out on Cleveland's Lake

Shore Boulevard. This establishment was fronted by a colorful gentleman named Louie Bleet, who proclaimed my engagement with an ad in the Cleveland *Plain Dealer* announcing my band as "Mickey Katz and His Pussies." This ad lasted *once;* then the embarrassed cooler heads at the *Plain Dealer* told him the ad was canceled.

But all Cleveland and Cuyahoga County had had a great laugh. For months jokesters around town would stop me on the street and say, "Mickey, I hear you've started a girls' band."

This early pussy job at Shore Acres was noteworthy for another reason: It nearly got me assassinated. The Shore Acres opening was a hot night, in more ways than one. High-flying gamblers and assorted bootleggers and classy hoodlums had come from all over the United States, to honor Louie on the opening of his new nightclub. As they came in, they all deposited their guns at the checkroom.

My trumpet player was my buddy Wizzle Rosenberg. Since it was a miserably humid night, Wizzle and I decided to walk down to the beach during a ten-minute break to get a breath of air. As we were on the stairs leading down to the water's edge, I got a poke in the ribs with a gun, and a voice with a *Little Caesar* accent said, "Where you goin', punks?"

I said, in a suddenly soprano voice, "We're just out to get a little air."

This character said, "Nobody comes down here to get air. Who the hell are you?"

I answered, "I'm Mickey Katz, the bandleader, and that's my trumpet player."

Another hood came over, took a look at me, and said, "Yeah, that's Mickey Katz. He's all right. Just go back and lead the goddamned band, Mickey, and from now on don't stick your nose in where it don't belong." Out on the lake we could see the lights of an approaching boat, arriving from Canada with a load of bootleg booze.

Yes, I'd played for the mob before. So when I got my job

leading the band at the Ohio Villa, I just played it straight
and didn't cause any trouble. I was the bandleader at the
Ohio Villa for about a year and a half. It was a magnificent
gambling palace. Our shows featured such stars as Lou
Holtz, Benny Fields and Blossom Seeley, Belle Baker, plus a
line of girls.

Then came a period in my career that I thoroughly enjoyed and will always treasure. With World War II under
way, impresario Herman Pirchner called me up from his
famous Alpine Village. This was a big Cleveland theater-
restaurant, at Seventeenth and Euclid, where Herman and
his brother Otto had long dispensed great Tyrolean food
and entertainment. They had the singing waiters with the
leather pants and the little hats with the feathers, and they
put on really outstanding operettas. The place was packed
all the time.

Then came World War II and Hitler. Suddenly anything
even faintly Germanic was suspect. By 1942 one yodel heard
from any American place of entertainment, and you might
just as well have put up a quarantine sign on the joint.

With their long-established Alpine Village in trouble,
Herman and Otto sent for me. They thought that having a
well-known Jewish musician leading their band might
take some of the anti-Nazi heat off them.

Well, I wanted no part of them if their sympathies were
in any way pro-Nazi, so I checked them out thoroughly. I
found that their attorney was my friend Herb Mendelsohn,
a very fine member of the Jewish community. Their banker
was Harry Cohen of the Morris Plan Bank—I was positive
he wasn't a Nazi sympathizer! The Pirchners even took
me down into the basement of the Alpine Village, and I
found that two of the chicken *flickers* (pluckers) were
Jewish refugees *from* Nazi Germany.

So I took the engagement and became Mickey Katz and
His Alpine Village Orchestra.

And almost immediately all hell broke loose. People
would turn in complaints that they'd seen known Bundists

walking into the Alpine Village, that Bund meetings were held there regularly, and the FBI would come over and shake us all down. I'll never forget one night when the local head of the FBI led a whole squadron of his men over to investigate us. When he didn't find any clandestine radios or storm troopers in the basement, he began grilling me and everyone in my orchestra. When he found out that my name was Katz and that my band was nearly all of Jewish or Italian ancestry—names like Rosenberg, Bogdanoff, Caputo, and Baldi—the head FBI man said to his troops, "What the hell are we doing here?" They put on their trench coats and retrenched, and that was our last visit from the FBI.

Then came what was to me the final proof of Herman Pirchner's bum rap: He was drafted into the United States Army! I became not only leader of the band, but now MC as well. Since Herman was no longer there to produce the operettas, we changed our format to the international type of vaudeville act—aerialists who rode the bicycles and performed other feats on the high wire, animal acts, great magicians. The agent who booked the acts was Frank Sennes, who later produced many top shows in Las Vegas and Hollywood.

Now perhaps you are wondering about my own draft status, what I personally did in the war. Well, I was not unknown in military circles. In fact, my first battlefront activity had occurred at the age of thirteen, when I took part in a city-wide tribute to the great French general and World War I hero Marshal Ferdinand Foch.

I had been playing my old Spanish-American-War clarinet about a year and a half when, in 1922, all Cleveland was excited by the news that there was going to be a downtown parade for Marshal Foch. And wonder of wonders, the ragtag and bobtail, sad sack, down-at-the-heels Central High School band was going to march in the parade! *I* would be marching, playing my clarinet! I told my folks, my relatives—I told everybody I knew—to be sure to come watch the parade and listen to my beautiful clarinet playing.

As I've already explained, Central High's idea of a really sharp band was to have two players with pants that matched. But to honor Marshal Foch, bandmaster Harry Clark decided to outdo himself. He searched Cleveland till he found some old World War I uniforms, the kind with the olive-drab cloth spiral puttees that you wrapped around your legs from ankles to knees. My uniform was naturally a hundred sizes too big for me; my chin hit the uniform where some soldier's *pupik* (naval) used to be. But I carefully rehearsed putting on the puttees.

The day of the parade! Dressed up like a soldier boy, I reported to the start of the parade route, at Twenty-third and Euclid Avenue, my heart thumping with pride and expectation.

Then, just as the parade was about to start, our first clarinetist, Frank Mateyka, broke his clarinet reed. Well, in those days reeds cost a whole nickel, so naturally nobody had a spare. And since I was the youngest and newest clarinet player in the band, Harry Clark took my reed and gave it to Frank!

So with my whole family watching, with all Cleveland watching, with the whole world watching, I went marching down Euclid Avenue, "playing" a reedless and tootless clarinet. And in the midst of this musical disaster, my puttees came loose and started unraveling behind me. There was no way I could stop to fix them, so I marched on, but not to glory. When the band marched past Sixth Street, the ends of my puttees were fluttering back around Eighteenth.

That was the start of my military career. From then on it got worse. When I got my draft notice and proudly reported for my preinduction physical in the early stages of World War II, the examining doctors greeted me with mirth. My small stature, my big glasses (which I wore at the time), my flatfeet, the problem of finding a rifle small enough for me to carry—everything about me aroused them to almost open hilarity. I finally received a 4-F, with four doctors joining in the laughter. I was rejected for the Army, the Navy, the Air Force, the Boy Scouts, the Girl Scouts, the Brownies, and the Junior B'nai B'rith.

Well, the hell with them. They'd had their chance. I would have to help win the war in other ways.

And I got the chance. After Herman Pirchner became a GI and I was leading the band and also acting as MC at the Alpine Village, I got a call from one of the priests at St. John's Cathedral. Like practically everybody else in Cleveland, he'd attended some of our Alpine Village shows, and he wondered if I could find the time to bring my band and some of our acts over to entertain the servicemen at the USO canteen at St. John's Cathedral. I said I certainly could —I relished the idea of a little Jewish boy entertaining the troops at the Catholic USO. I entertained over there for many months. Today St. John's Cathedral is more than a hundred years old, but it's still at Ninth and Superior. It was my privilege to contribute to its USO efforts during the war.

That reminds me of an old Jewish gentleman who was a patient in a Catholic hospital. The nuns and doctors took excellent care of him; when he was leaving to go home, well and strong again, he said, "You have treated me so fine, is there anything I can do? I would like to contribute something."

The head of the hospital said, "Well, now that you ask, we need ten thousand dollars."

The Jewish gentleman asked, "What's the purpose?"

"We need twenty new urinals in the interns' quarters."

"You got it." The grateful old man wrote out a check for ten thousand dollars and went home.

When he got home, his equally grateful wife said, "The Catholics were beautiful to you, Sam. I hope you gave them something for their hospital."

He said, "I certainly did. I gave them ten thousand dollars."

"What's the purpose?"

"They are needing twenty new urinals."

She asked, "What's a urinal?"

The old man answered, "How the hell do I know? I'm not a Catholic."

The next week, after arranging to take some entertainment to St. John's USO canteen, I got a call from the Treasury Department. During the shows at the Alpine Village could I sell a few war bonds? Again I certainly could.

From then on every night at the end of each show I would say, "Ladies and gentlemen, we're sitting here eating great food and enjoying a great show. Our husbands and fathers and brothers are over there in the mud, putting their lives on the line. Even as I make this announcement, more of them are getting killed. Let's get this war over with and bring them home!" Every week I sold at least $25,000 or $30,000 worth of war bonds. I received a public citation from the Treasury Department.

Then, in the summer of 1945, I got an unusual chance to help to win what was left of the war.

At that time New York City was jammed with troops—troops on their way to the Pacific, other thousands of soldiers standing around trying to find out where the hell they were going. And they all were looking for an evening of fun and relaxation.

The current craze in the music business was the little comedy bands—the Korn Kobblers, the Hoosier Hotshots, Al Trace. So I organized a little six-man comedy group called Mickey Katz and His Krazy Kittens. Again I hired the best musicians, and we had a great group of entertainers. My agent in Cleveland—Stan Zucker—immediately booked us into New York's Aquarium Restaurant.

The Aquarium Restaurant, we were told, was "doing something for the boys." When we got there, we found out what it was doing for "the boys" was to separate them from their money as fast as possible. The Aquarium had four different bands that blasted away in shifts twenty-four hours a day, pausing only long enough for the cops and the MPs to drag away drunk GIs and teenage prostitutes. Those poor GIs were really getting rocked and rolled.

Playing in this den of GI iniquity, I was trying to figure out a way to get out of my contract when who walked in one night but movie star Betty Hutton. Accompanying her was Abe Lastfogel, head of the prestigious William Morris talent agency. They had heard on the Broadway grapevine that I had a great little band, and they had fought their way in for a listen. Betty was looking for a musical group to take with her on a USO tour to entertain the troops overseas. She listened to us play two numbers, then ran up to the bandstand, threw her arms around me, and said, "I love you! Please be my band!"

For the worthy purpose of the USO trip the Aquarium let us out of our contract. For the trip the USO made me a temporary officer, with a little "chicken" (colonel's eagle) on my overseas cap. Wearing my beautiful trench coat, I walked proudly up Broadway, feeling like a regular Robert Mitchum.

At first we didn't know where we were going, and seemingly, neither did the Army. They gave us shots for the Pacific.

So the next day we left for Europe.

I had never been on a plane in my life, and ours was a wartime propeller-driven bucket-seat job. Aboard were Betty Hutton, Mickey Katz and His Scared Kittens, a comedian named Johnny Morgan, a dancer named Bea Wayne, and about twenty newspaper correspondents from America's leading newspapers, heading for various foreign assignments.

Our plane took off at about one-thirty in the morning. A few hours later we were flying along in the moonlight when I noticed that one of our engines was on fire. I woke up my piano player, Lenny, who had told me he was an experienced flier. He was half asleep—and half drunk. He took a look out the window at the blazing motor and said, "Don't worry, they're testing the engines." And he went back to sleep. I was about to go to sleep when the thought hit me: They're testing the engines *up here?* The crew finally used an automatic fire extinguisher on the flaming engine, and the flames stopped. So did the engine. The sergeant who was acting as steward in the cabin told us not to worry; we could get along fine on three of our four motors.

Then one of the motors on the other side caught fire! Sparks and flame were all over the wing, which even I knew was full of gasoline. They stopped this other flaming engine and shot the fire extinguisher on it. Now we were operating on two wings and a prayer, which, even combined, wasn't enough. I again woke up my piano player, Lenny. He stared out blearily at the two stopped propellers and said, "Look at the cheap bastards—saving gas!"

Everybody on the plane was either sick or too scared to get sick. The sergeant-steward came in again and said, "Ladies and gentlemen, we have a serious problem. We think we can stay up with the two engines that are still operating. Luckily, there's one on each side." I thought, how lucky can you get! And then I threw up.

But the sergeant continued to talk. "We're still about two hundred and fifty miles from the Azores, but if we don't have any more trouble, we should make it in about an hour and a half."

Well, we made it. We landed with our wheels practically in the water, with a beach full of fire engines awaiting our arrival. But we made it. As we scrambled out of the plane, a bright young Special Services officer was there to greet us. He saluted Betty Hutton smartly and said, "Miss Hutton, we will have you back in the air in a new plane in fifteen minutes."

Miss Hutton said, "You can take your new plane and stick it up your ass." Then she marched to the camp, crawled into a cot, closed her mosquito netting, and didn't get up for a day and a half.

We finally flew on over to Paris. Betty Hutton checked in at the Hotel Ritz, the correspondents went to their press quarters, and the rest of us went to a beautiful old château outside Paris. I entertained the French chambermaids by making funny faces at them, and in two days they were calling me *le petit comique.*

Then we started doing an endless succession of USO camp shows—thousands of soldiers waiting for our show at each camp and wild yells of appreciation when we were finished.

I'll say one thing for Betty Hutton, and the reason I remember it is that it nearly destroyed my little kosher stomach. At all the camps Betty refused to eat with the officers, so we always ate with the GIs, and what the GIs were eating in those disordered days was ham and beans. It may be psychological, but I have never been able to digest ham or pork. But it was either eat ham or starve, so I ate ham for Uncle Sam. Plus becoming bloated from the steady diet of gassy beans, I sort of floated on and off the stage like a toy blimp. But the troops liked the show, and that is what counts. We played to individual audiences of as many as eighty thousand men.

And between shows I saw events so tragic as to wring your heart. In an old section of Paris I found five hundred Jewish refugees living in an abandoned warehouse. They were drinking hot water because they had no tea to put in the hot water. Led by Betty Hutton, we stormed the PX and liberated a fifty-pound case of tea for them.

Another time, in Reims, a Jewish chaplain at one of the camps passed the word that on Friday night a synagogue that the Nazis had blown apart with cannon fire and later used as a stable was to be reopened. Would I join the congregation?

That night, *Shabbes* night, there were seven hundred American Jewish GIs at the synagogue. There were exactly *eight* former members of the synagogue in attendance, eight Jews who were still alive because they had been hidden by their gentile friends in the farmhouses outside town for four years! One pathetic old man kept asking me if I knew a David Cohen in America. Mr. Cohen was the old man's son; if he could find his son, he might send for him. That evening broke my heart.

By the time we had worked our way down to Marseille, Hutton was getting worn out emotionally, and she was missing a lot of shows. The shows where she did appear she killed them. She was a fabulous performer and a tremendous talent.

A funny thing happened when we got to Marseille. The Army guide assigned to us was comedian Phil Foster. Phil was getting along about as well with Army discipline as you might imagine. He'd started out as a sergeant, but he'd been rapidly knocked down to corporal and more recently to private. Phil's trouble was that he sort of ran his own war. The second day he was our guide he said, "How would you like some doughnuts and ice cream?" After our weeks of ham and beans the thought was so exciting that we could hardly speak. Phil said to stop stammering and get him a jeep out of the motor pool. We drove about fifteen miles out into the countryside, to a farmhouse where a bunch of German prisoners who were master bakers and cooks were busy making ice cream and doughnuts for the brass.

Phil walked in as though he were General Patton. He said, "Give me gee-kuchen twelve duzen doughnuts and gee-faltzen six gallons of ice cream. And be quick about it, or I'll have your *tochis!*" Phil might have been a private, but he talked like a general. The German bakers and ice-cream makers hurried to fill his order. We went back to our hotel in Marseille and had a feast. We even treated the chambermaids.

Then suddenly it was V-J Day, the war in the Pacific was mercifully over, and all the troops billeted around Marseille waiting to be shipped out for Japan went wild with relief and happiness. They understandably proceeded to rip up Marseille. You couldn't buy whiskey because there wasn't any, but the French made a lethal liquid called calvados, which was a fruit booze guaranteed to render you blotto in no time at all. The deliriously happy American troops hit the calvados, and in a few hours Marseille was a wildly drunk town.

In the midst of this I decided that this would be a good time to go shopping downtown and buy Grace a nice bottle of Chanel perfume!

I barely escaped with my life. Thousands of drunk GIs were breaking store windows in their exuberance, with the MPs doing their best to keep the situation from turning into a real riot. And who is this shmucky colonel making his way through the pandemonium? That was me, Colonel Katz!

A funny thing happened on my way to the Chanel boutique. As I passed one off-limits saloon, trying to be as unobtrusive as possible, a couple of drunk GIs were hurled out into the street. They picked themselves up off the sidewalk and turned and saw me, in my full regalia, with phony "chicken" on my overseas cap. One of them said, "Christ, it's the Old Man!" Meaning the real colonel. They both snapped to attention. As I answered their weaving salute, it was the proudest moment of my entire military career.

One final war note: When I got home from Europe, I had a strange itching around my groin. It felt like some loathsome venereal disease. But if a venereal bug had got me, it must have flown in the window. However, I did my best not to get too close to Grace and the kids. Grace looked at me a little oddly.

So I went secretly to an expensive dermatologist, one unknown to the family. He made about a hundred tests, then announced, "You do not have syphilis." Well, that was a relief.

"What you have," he went on pontifically, "is a nerve disease called *lichen planus*." (I kid you not.) He gave me

a prescription for shots I would have to take. I had meanwhile been booked for an engagement playing and leading
my comedy band at the Glenn Rendezvous, which was one
of the largest gambling spas at Newport, Kentucky, across
the river from Cincinnati. I went down there, played for
the gamblers, itched, and took my shots for *lichen planus*.
The needle was longer than the name of the disease.

In the meantime, Grace and the kids back home started
to itch. With no need for secrecy, Grace took them to our
family dermatologist. He examined them and said, "What
you've all got is scabies—a little parasite that burrows under
your skin and drives you nuts. Mickey must have picked
it up in one of those wartime European hotels." Grace
called me in Kentucky, we all slapped on a little simple
sulphur ointment, and that was the end of *lichen planus*.

When I got back to Cleveland, I gave *my* dermatologist
what was left of my sulphur ointment. I will not tell you
where I gave it to him.

And that, Joel and Ronnie, is what Daddy did in the war.

6 · City Slickers and Shikkers

Do you remember Spike Jones and His City Slickers? Remember the Slicker doing the glugs and other comical throat sounds on "Cocktails for Two," "Holiday for Strings," and the "Hawaiian War Chant"?

That was me.

I first met Spike Jones in March of 1946. When I had arrived back in Cleveland after my USO tour of Europe, for at least a week I proudly wore my uniform around town. The newspapers took my picture, and the captions said, "Mickey Katz Returns from the War." I walked up and down Euclid Avenue, saluting everybody, but nobody saluted back. My military act was finished.

Then my friend accordionist Joe Baldi said, "Mickey, we've seen the suit already." So I regretfully put the suit away among my souvenirs and started looking for work.

After the Glenn Rendezvous engagement down at Newport, Kentucky, and a tour of Syracuse and Dayton, I finally arrived back in Cleveland "for good" toward the end of February 1946.

I shortly got a call from Jack Cohen, head of the jukebox association for the state of Ohio. He was planning a national jukebox convention to be held in Cleveland, and Jack wanted me to conduct the orchestra and the acts for the show.

Since it was a jukebox convention, the show naturally featured a lot of big record names and big acts. The biggest was Spike Jones and His City Slickers, at the time the hottest record and road attraction in the country. His smash-hit recording of "Der Fuehrer's Face," which came out at the start of World War II when the whole free world wanted desperately to lampoon Hitler, had vaulted Spike Jones into superstardom. By 1946, after a string of hit records, he was an American institution.

After I conducted the jukebox show, including playing some clarinet solos, I met Spike backstage. He complimented me on my clarinet work, and I did some of my throat glugs for him.

A week later I got a telegram from the Coast: DEAR MICKEY. WOULD YOU AND YOUR GLUGS LIKE TO JOIN ME IN HOLLYWOOD? SPIKE.

He started me at $175 a week, which I thought was a nothing salary, since I would have to send money home to Grace and the kids and pay my own expenses on the road. But I didn't care what money he paid me to start; Spike Jones was such a hot attraction that I wanted to be with him. And I had no doubt of my ability to become so important to him that my salary would rapidly increase. Oh, boy! Was I wrong!

When I arrived in Hollywood, Spike couldn't have been more cordial. The first night he invited me to dinner at his home on Roxbury Drive in Beverly Hills. His wife, Pat, and his eight-year-old daughter, Linda, were charming. A few days later Spike took Linda on a trip to Las Vegas; he invited me to go along, all expenses paid, and I had a ball. No man could have been a more gracious host than Spike Jones.

As a matter of fact, Spike and I always had a cordial relationship, even later when we got into the weird discussions about money. He was a fine musician—he'd started out as a great drummer for John Scott Trotter—and we always had complete musical respect for each other. We both wanted to play only one way—good.

To understand how strange it was that he refused to pay me a decent salary, you must understand a few more things about our relationship. I thought I was more important to him in the production of the show than most of his other musicians, great as they were. And believe me, they were great. But in addition to my clarinet solos and comedy specialties. I conducted the other acts of the show when Spike wasn't onstage. Spike also discussed comedy arrangements and special lyrics with me.

But even more than this were our close personal ties. Since neither one of us hit the bottle—I never had, and Spike had taken the oath—I was a little different from some of the unmarried *shikkers* (tipplers) in his band. On the road I occasionally lived with him in his suites in the hotels when we'd be playing a city for a week's theater engagement.

My wife, Grace, and Spike's wife, Pat, even became good friends. They went into business together making hats— Grace & Pat, Millinery. (Grace managed to get top billing.)

And even with all this, when I'd suggest to Spike that it wouldn't be too expensive if he'd give me a raise of a couple dollars, he'd flatly refuse. He finally raised me to $225 a week; anything beyond that he considered ridiculous. This at a time when we were playing big auditoriums all over the country and he was taking in as much as $10,000 a day. I once said to him, "Spike, in your tax bracket you could give me a raise of five hundred dollars a week, and it wouldn't cost you a hundred."

He said, "I know, but I don't want to spend the hundred."

With Spike, money was to have, not to spend. He considered the spending of money not only sinful, but stupid. I once went into a restaurant with him in Philadelphia. I gave my hat to the hatcheck girl, and when we got to our table, Spike, who was hatless, said, "Mickey, you'll never have any money."

"What do you mean?"

"Why do you wear the hat?"

"Because my head gets cold."

"Well, why give it to the hatcheck girl and waste a tip? Why don't you park it under your chair?"

Spike never carried any money with him. If he needed $2 for something, he'd borrow it from you. He'd pay it back when his business office in Beverly Hills sent him his "allowance." He had a personal manager who traveled with us and collected all the proceeds and sent it to the business office out on the Coast.

His personal manager's system with the money worked fine till we got to Elko, Nevada, a typical western cowboy town. Bing Crosby's ranch was nearby. One night a playful rancher came to the show with a barrel of silver dollars and upended the barrel, showering them all over the place. We performed on the flat floor because there was no stage. When the rain of silver dollars started, everybody in Spike's band forgot about the show and started scrambling for the silver dollars.

But our closing night was one I will never forget. Since it was Nevada, the hotel operators paid our business manager the week's receipts in cash—some $18,000. The business manager put the money in his inside coat pocket in a manila envelope and went across the street to the Stockmen's Hotel, which served great steaks.

It also served great drinks. Gradually a bunch of the ranchers and sheepherders joined our man, and he got gloriously drunk.

The business manager happened to be rooming with me. At five o'clock in the morning I was in bed asleep when he finally came banging in. "Hiya, Mick, old boy, old boy," he said.

He started to undress, put his hand in his inner pocket where he'd had the money . . . and suddenly he froze. "The money," he cried. "I've lost the money!" He sobered up in about a second and a half because he knew this would be difficult to explain to Spike, on two counts: not only the money, but I've seen Spike fire one of his best performers on the spot for appearing onstage loaded.

I got up and dressed, took the trembling manager in tow, and we went back over to the Stockmen's Hotel. That's where our man had spent the whole evening; he said he'd never left the bar.

At the hotel bar, nobody had turned in any manila envelope. We searched the lobby—no trace of the money. And there really wasn't any place else in Elko he could have gone.

All he could do was to go back and tell Spike, then shoot himself.

As we passed the desk on the way out, the night desk clerk said to our business manager, "Are you checking out now?" The manager looked at him blankly, puzzled. Then he remembered. Oh, yes, he told me, when he'd got so loaded that he didn't want to take a chance on coming home and running into Spike, he'd got a room at the Stockmen's Motel and fallen into bed.

We rushed up to the room, and there, under the pillow, was the manila envelope with the $18,000.

Spike never found out it had been lost.

Let me tell you something about the compassionate side of Spike Jones. I had been with the show only three or four weeks when my brother, Al, called me in Seattle to tell me that Mama had suffered a heart seizure and was not expected to live. I asked Spike to advance me some money so I could fly home. With no hesitation he wrote a note to his business manager to give me several hundred dollars, and he said to come back when I could.

This was the spring of 1946, and there were hundreds of thousands of discharged servicemen trying to get here and there around the country. There was no such thing as a direct flight from Seattle to Cleveland, or even a reasonable indirect flight. Desperate to get home to see my mother before it was too late, I got on a flight down to Los Angeles.

I had an emergency ticket, but it wasn't much help. I waited at the Los Angeles airport for six or eight hours; then I got a flight to Oklahoma City. From there I got a plane to Chicago. I had now been trying to get home for some thirty hours. After a wait in Chicago for another four hours, I finally got a flight on to Cleveland, where my brother, Al, and several of my cousins were waiting for me at the airport.

Al rushed me home, where my mother was in an oxygen tent. She hadn't been expected to survive till my arrival, but with a firmness of soul she had waited to see me. As I came into the room, she threw off the oxygen tent and grasped me in an encompassing embrace. Exhausted from this emotional moment, she almost immediately went into a sound sleep. The doctor came to the house a half hour later, and said. "Mama looks much better now. I have great hopes for her recovery."

But the next morning about eight o'clock she died.

We buried my mother on Mother's Day. On the way from the funeral home on One Hundred and Fifth Street to the cemetery, the funeral cortege stopped in front of our family's Orthodox synagogue. The doors of the synagogue were flung open, and as the procession stopped there opposite the open doors of her synagogue, God accepted my mother's soul. To this day I cry when I think about that tragic day.

A week later I rejoined Spike. During the rest of the tour I said Kaddish (the Jewish mourner's prayer) every day on the Spike Jones train. When we got into a town, I would find out if there was a synagogue and if a service was to be held that day so I could say Kaddish there. In small towns this can be a problem. To hold a service in a synagogue requires a *minyan* (a quorum of ten men). Ten Jewish men can hold a religious service in a synagogue, in anyone's home, or out in a field.

But how do you assemble ten men for a weekday religious service in a small town where there are maybe only a

hundred Jewish families altogether? The men are in business; they're working; they can't come to the synagogue
every day. So they take turns, and thus ten men assemble
every day to form a *minyan* so they can hold a service.

In many small towns, as I found out when I was touring
with Spike, the local rabbi was also the cantor, the *mohel*
(who performed the circumcisions), the teacher in the
Hebrew school, and he might also run the town's kosher
butcher shop.

I learned one thing in my visits to small and large
synagogues all across this country: All the Jewish people
don't live in New York, Beverly Hills, and Miami. There
must have been a lot of our people in those covered wagons
heading west because today there are Jewish communities
throughout the West.

I must tell you a little about "the Spike Jones train." We
traveled in two Pullman cars, which they shunted off onto
sidings at the towns where we played. We were on that
train sometimes continuously for as many as fifty dates. If
you had fifty one-night stands with Spike, they were con-
secutive; no time off. When we needed a bath, we went to
the YMCA. That was a crazy train. Comic Doodles Weaver
had a picture of Christ tacked up in his berth; it was
autographed "To Doodles—from J.C." We froze on that
train, and nearly drowned. One night late I looked out the
window, and we were going through a flood, nothing but
water as far as you could see. But later that day we pulled
into some farm town and played a show at the local Grange
Hall to 3,000 people.

Those were tough days. We had a New York carnival
hustler in charge of selling the "Spike Jones Souvenir
Program." This man had diabetes. He had an attack one
day when the train was about to pull out, and he collapsed
across the track back of the train at the station. The train
pulled out and left him there.

Spike Jones must have been a great man because he attracted so many great people to him. George Rock was a fabulous trumpet player, but he will always be remembered as the big fellow in the childish nightgown who sang "All I Want for Christmas Is My Two Front Teeth." Red Ingle made Spike's record of "Chloe" famous. Dick Morgan was the master of the chicken and other barnyard sounds; "Dr. Horatio Birdbath" did the bird whistles.

And they were all great musicians. Including the girl "harpist" who sat at the side of the stage through the whole show, knitting the endless muffler we called the rug. At the end of each show she played just *one* note, but it was a great note! That's the way Spike worked.

Being a perfectionist, he was always looking for new talent. Or it might be more accurate to say that new talent was always looking for him. He picked up Kaye Ballard in Cleveland; she was an usherette at the Palace Theater when we played there in the summer of 1946, but she already had the makings of a star. She got an audition with Spike, and he hired her on the spot, to sing and do her terrific impressions. Freddie Morgan was discovered in much the same way. Freddie was the great banjo player who performed the "banjo concerto" on "The World Is Waiting for the Sunrise." Spike hired Freddie on my say-so without an audition.

While I was with Spike, he also discovered vocalist Helen Grayco, in Tacoma, Washington. Her parents were well-to-do Italian-Americans and devout Catholics; they were fine people. Helen was seventeen and the prettiest little thing you ever saw. The minute Spike heard her sing—and looked at her—he hired her. At the Tacoma railroad station, when she was leaving to go with us on tour, her mother drew Kaye Ballard aside; since Kaye was also Italian, Helen's mother asked her in Italian to take care of her baby, Helen.

Kaye tried to be Helen's chaperone, but it didn't do a hell of a lot of good. After we were on the road for a little while and it was apparent that Spike was falling for Helen,

Kaye drew Helen aside one day and did her best to warn her about life and Spike. After all, he's a married man, etc., etc.

Helen evidently reported the conversation to Spike. From then on he never spoke to Kaye Ballard. He wouldn't even conduct for her; I had to conduct her numbers.

But nobody could say that Spike's intentions weren't honorable. He divorced his first wife, Pat, and married Helen Grayco; after having had one child with Pat, he had three more children with Helen. Spike Jones and Helen Grayco became America's Sweethearts. Her folks moved down to Los Angeles from Tacoma, and Spike invested money with them in very successful food markets in the Los Angeles area. It was an idyllic situation.

But there was a shadow hanging over them. Spike had long suffered from emphysema. He died—much too young—when he simply ran out of breath.

Today Helen, wealthy in her own right, is married to Bill Rosen, who owns the prestigious Gatsby's Restaurant in Brentwood in West Los Angeles. Bill and Helen and Helen's brother and sisters all help run the restaurant. Spike Jones, Jr., now in his middle twenties, is just starting out in show business.

I'll never forget Spike Jones. He was a complex and little-understood man. One time when we were playing the Trocadero on Hollywood's famed Sunset Strip, Spike spent a lot of money and hired about thirty extra musicians, fine ones, to have himself a symphonic jazz orchestra like Paul Whiteman. Conducting his symphonic orchestra, Spike was in seventh heaven. No funny stuff, just beautiful music.

And do you know what the crowds who came in, said? They said, "What kind of crap is this? If we want a symphony, we'll go to Hollywood Bowl. We came to hear Spike Jones, not Stokowski."

Maybe if Spike had never made that first funny record, who knows? . . .

After I was with Spike for about a year and a half, I told

him he'd have to raise me to at least $350. He said he couldn't, he wouldn't, and he didn't. So I left.

And suddenly here was Mickey Katz, super-clarinetist and saxophonist, talented conductor, star of hilarious comedy bits. So how come I wasn't working? I was a married man with two children and no job. I was beginning to wonder if life really began at forty.

I needn't have worried. I was a late bloomer, but thank God I was about to bloom.

7· Hold That Tiger, Hal Zeiger

LIFE FOR ME didn't really begin at forty. It began at thirty-eight. I beat the clock by two years.

Nineteen forty-seven was a very important year for me. I left Spike Jones, faced starvation, decided not to starve, and a month later recorded my first English-Yiddish comedy record.

Here's how it happened:

Exactly when you get a big idea is usually hard to pin down. An idea that changes your whole life is usually the culmination of a lot of little happenings that gradually form a pattern. When I was still a teenager and playing in Doc Whipple's big band at the Golden Pheasant Chinese Restaurant in Cleveland, we had a radio pickup every night over WTAM, the NBC station in Cleveland. As part of the radio show, I began making up and performing English-Yiddish parodies of the well-known bedtime stories. These Katz Klassics included "Little Red Rosenberg," "Hanzel end Ganzel," and "Yoshke and the Beanstalk." They proved so popular that I collected them into a little book entitled *Nonzense on Who's Whoo end Wat's Wat*. This distinguished volume had a wide sale in Cleveland and cost me several hundred dollars, the problem being that I sold them for $1 a copy and found out later they were costing me $1.25. Plus the fact that the illustrations were done by my teenage Cousin Bernie, and Bernie's father sued me for his son's share of "the profits." Which weren't.

But at least the book and my bedtime stories over the radio were enhancing my reputation as a funnyman. From then on I was always part musician and part comedian. And then came the year 1947, after I'd left Spike. One of my last tasks for Spike Jones was a recording session at the RCA recording studio on Sycamore in Hollywood. When Spike had a recording session, like most recording artists, he hired extra musicians to embellish the band. And for this particular session one of the extra musicians he hired was the great trumpet virtuoso Mannie Klein. Since Mannie and I were the only *landsmen* (co-religionists) in the band, during a ten-minute break I told Mannie a few Jewish jokes.

He said, "Mickey, I'll bet you could do a funny Yiddish parody record." As a matter of fact, I'd already written one, and I sang "Haim afen Range" for Mannie and the boys. What I didn't know was that the mike into the control room was open, so "the boys" who were hearing it included Walt Hebner, head of A & R (Artists & Repertory) for RCA, and RCA's big record boss from New York, Eli Oberstein. I finally noticed them on the other side of the glass, laughing up a storm.

Now at the same time a couple of English-Yiddish comedy records had already come out, sung by the Barton Brothers. They were original numbers done in combined song and monologue. The first one was called "Joe and Paul," about two guys who ran a comedy clothing store on the Lower East Side. Their follow-up record was "Cockeyed Jennie," about a middle-aged lady of the evening. The gist of "Cockeyed Jennie" was a father who was distressed over his son's pimples; in desperation he took the boy to see Jennie. After a few of Jennie's "treatments," the lad's pimples cleared up like magic. (It is not known whether "Cockeyed Jennie" was the inspiration for the later book and movie *Portnoy's Complaint*.) The Barton Brothers' records were recorded by a small company, but they were a big hit in the major cities where there were sizable Jewish communities.

At any rate, a couple of months after I left Spike all these events conspired to give me an idea. I suddenly saw the possibilities of writing and recording English-Yiddish parodies of *all* the current crop of hit tunes, similar to my chance parody of "Home on the Range." I called up Walt Hebner at RCA, told him of my plans, and asked him if he'd like to start things off by recording "Haim afen Range." Hebner said he'd call Oberstein in New York and get back to me. Oberstein, aware of the success of the Barton Brothers' records, said, "Go!"

Now I needed a second tune for the flip side. So I wrote the lyrics to "Yiddish Square Dance," in which I impersonate an Arkansas hog caller calling a square dance in Yiddish.

For the music I went to my friend Al Sack, who was the musical director for the network radio shows of Tony Martin and Dinah Shore. Al liked the lyrics and thought that recording the numbers might be fun. So he wrote a melody for "Yiddish Square Dance" and sketched out a musical background for "Haim afen Range."

Now I needed musicians. I didn't know any of the top musicians in Hollywood other than Mannie Klein. Al Sack naturally did, and he proceeded to assemble for me a band that included Mannie Klein on trumpet, Sammy Weiss on drums, Benny Gill on violin, Si Zentner on trombone, Wally Wechsler on piano, and Nat Farber as arranger, a Who's Who of the greatest jazz musicians in Hollywood. They all agreed to make the recording because the numbers reminded them of the songs their parents had enjoyed. To them, making the recording was like playing a bar mitzvah. I called the band Mickey Katz and His Kosher Jammers.

When RCA heard the record, they rushed out ten thousand copies and shot them off to New York City. At that

time, 1947, all the Times Square and Broadway record
stores—dozens of them from Forty-second Street up to Fifty-
fifth—had loudspeakers out on the sidewalk, blaring out the
most popular records. When my record arrived in New
York, the Jewish record store owners immediately put it on
the outside loudspeakers, and suddenly hundreds of thousands of New Yorkers started hearing "Haim afen Range"
and "Yiddish Square Dance" by Mickey Katz.

In three days the stores sold out the original ten thousand
records and took orders for twenty-five thousand more!
RCA got its record presses in Scranton rolling. The sales
kept booming along on the East Coast—New York, Boston,
Hartford, Philadelphia and Baltimore—and then the record
started rolling west. An old Central High School classmate,
Art Newman, had a big record store in Cleveland; he sold
so many of my first record that he called me up in Hollywood to thank me for all the business I was bringing into
his store.

A fabulous guy named Little Al had a big record and
appliance store in Chicago; he sold so many copies of
"Haim afen Range" that he almost forgot to sell any refrig-
erators. Then the record rolled on west to Los Angeles, and
it was suddenly selling great in Boyle Heights and in
Norty's Music Store on Fairfax Avenue.

The next step, naturally, was a second record. "Tico,
Tico" was a huge hit then, so I made an English-Yiddish
version called "Tickle, Tickle," backed by "Chloya," my
version of "Chloe." On "Chloya" I did a Yiddish imitation
of the Ink Spots that tickled my new fans. The second
record sold even bigger than the first one, meaning like
latkes at a Hadassah breakfast.

With the success of the second record, I felt that I'd
proved that I had something. I had given the Jewish record-
buying public something that they evidently wanted and
up to now hadn't had. I knew that all over America there
must be thousands of record buyers who would like to see
me in person.

But I had no idea how to go about it.

At this point the Man Upstairs dialed my phone in the person of Hal Zeiger. I had known Hal since he was a saxophone player and orchestra leader in Cleveland. During World War II Hal was a military flight instructor; he'd written a book on civil aviation that had become a bible of the industry. After the war Hal Zeiger had become a very important artists' agent in Hollywood. He'd booked Ray Charles, Erroll Garner, Moms Mabley, plus the Three Redheads, one of whom was Dick Van Dyke. Hal said to come over to his offices on the Sunset Strip and we'd talk.

Hal Zeiger was to be my manager and partner for twenty years. I could write four books about him. Like most partnerships that are successful, Hal and I are complete opposites. I give him an E for Effort, a G for Guts, and a B for Brilliance. He's a big ballsy guy about six feet two; he'd walk up to a bull elephant and hit him right in the eye.

Hal's first move as my manager was to call up Milt Krasny, then vice-president of GAC, General Artists Corporation. Milt booked such star talent as Perry Como, the Dorsey Brothers. . . .

As it happened, I also knew Milt Krasny very well. His mother and my mother had been dear friends in Cleveland; they'd gone to Mothers' Camp together. I knew Milt, his wife, his brother, and his sisters.

In Cleveland, Milt Krasny was always a very personable man and a great politician. He'd started out as a violinist; then he'd become an attorney. When the Depression hit in the early thirties, he became a starving attorney. I talked Maurice Spitalny into giving him a job on violin in our orchestra at the Palace. After I'd talked to Maurice about him for a while, Maurice said, "Okay, he has a family to support, I'll hire him."

Around 1937 Krasny ran for president of the Cleveland Musicians Union; he defeated Otto Kapl for the post. Milt was president of the Cleveland Musicians Union for four years, and during this time he used his position to good

effect. He ingratiated himself with the huge Music Corporation of America and every other musical corporation
with lots of clout. He stopped being a musician and became one of the bosses—as VP of the General Artists Corporation. When GAC went out of business, Milt Krasny
became one of Sinatra's managers, a job he holds today.

But in 1947 Hal and I needed Milt Krasny for a booking.

At that time the Los Angeles Jewish people had begun
migrating west to Fairfax Avenue, but there was still a
large Jewish community on the east side of Los Angeles,
called Boyle Heights. There was also a large Mexican-
American population near there. The only big theater
nearby that had stage shows was the Million Dollar Theater
in downtown Los Angeles. Krasny figured that with my
Jewish records, plus my parody takeoff on the great Latin
hit "Tico, Tico," I ought to kill 'em at the Million Dollar.
So he booked me and my great little band, including
trumpeter Max Herman, now president of the Los Angeles
Musicians Union, for a week's engagement at the Million
Dollar Theater.

Krasny was right. I was a double-ethnic smash. The
Jewish people would yell, "Hey, Mickele, play a *frailach*
[an old-country happy Jewish wedding dance]!" The Mexican people didn't understand my Yiddish lyrics on "Tickle,
Tickle" (my version of "Tico, Tico"), but they loved our
Latin rhythm and my antics onstage during my singing of
the number. So I was also a favorite of the Mexican patrons.

That reminds me of a wonderful anecdote about that
engagement. There was a music store on Brooklyn Avenue
in Boyle Heights named the Phillips Music Company. The
clientele was combined Jewish and Mexican, like my fans
at the Million Dollar. Bill Phillips told me that one day
two little Mexican girls came in. They said they wanted
that new record of "Tico, Tico." The clerk asked if they
wanted the "Tico, Tico" by Xavier Cugat. No. The one
by Tito Puentes? No. The one by Miguelito Valdez? No.
But this struck a nerve. One of the little girls said, "I

know—we want the one by Miguelito Katz."

After my bagel-and-bongos triumph at the Million Dollar, Hal and Krazny next booked me into Slapsie Maxie's, the huge new ultrafancy night club on the Wilshire Miracle Mile in West Los Angeles.

This was a distinctly different situation. In a way the Million Dollar had been a plain-plain preliminary bout; Slapsie Maxie's was the fancy-fancy main event. The place was named, naturally, for "Slapsie Maxie" Rosenbloom, the great Jewish fighter who "slapped" his opponents into submission rather than knocking them stiff like Joe Louis. When Maxie's fighting days ended, he started a very successful second career as a nightclub comic telling dirty jokes. The first club named for him, the original Slapsie Maxie's, was a tiny place holding maybe a hundred people at Beverly Boulevard and La Brea in Hollywood. One of the other acts there was a young comic named Jackie Gleason.

The original little Slapsie Maxie's was such a hit that plans were shortly afoot to open a much bigger place. Owner Sam Lewis built a big new Slapsie Maxie's out on Wilshire Boulevard, a big theater-restaurant seating maybe six hundred. Then Sammy shortly sold it to the Devore Brothers, one of whom was Sy Devore, the famous tailor and haberdasher to many of the Hollywood stars.

The big new Slapsie Maxie's was successful right from the opening night. Among the great acts that played there were Martin & Lewis, comic Joe E. Louis, Sophie Tucker. . . . Every night in the audience there were more stars than you can see on a clear night in Arizona. Slapsie Maxie's was the big leagues; you either got really famous fast, or you fell on your ass fast.

And out on that big stage one night walked little Mickey Katz, backed by my little Million Dollar band and singing my two record hits in my cowboy outfit with "Bar Mitzvah Ranch" plastered across it. To make sure that the audience was getting its money's worth, I also did some of my early non-Yiddish comedy numbers, including my imitation of an Italian lady opera star singing "Il Bacio," with electric bulbs in the tits that lit up when I hit the high notes.

I have some unforgettable memories of that first show at Slapsie Maxie's. Dan Dailey sat looking up at me as though I'd gone crazy; his frozen stare said, "What the hell is this?" But Perry Como, an old friend from back in Cleveland, applauded lustily. As a matter of fact, most of the audience applauded; but others looked pained. All in all, I had the feeling that I wasn't being everybody's glass of tea with lemon.

As soon as the first show was over, I found out with great speed that my hunch was correct. Owner-manager Sy Devore arrived at my dressing room so mad he was trembling. He said, "I will not have this! There will be no Yiddish done in this club! Get that through your head right now!" And he stormed out.

When Hal came to my dressing room a few moments later, I told him what had happened. His answer was typical. He said, "Up his lazy river—straight ahead, Mick."

What I did was to avoid the Devores for the next few nights, while I continued to do my act. The Yiddish lyrics were admittedly a problem to those in the audience who didn't understand Yiddish.

Spike Jones came in one night; after the show he came to my dressing room and said, "I enjoyed the show, but don't you think you should supply a libretto (an English translation)?"

But the audience enjoyed our comedy and fun, including the parodies. The late Walter Winchell said one day in his column: "Mickey Katz is the only funny Jewish comedian in show biz." I treasure that, because Winchell realized what I was trying to do—an American Jewish show for everybody, with a sprinkling of Yiddish words to please my special audience.

But let me tell you, it was slow going. I remember in the early fifties, even after I'd been a proved recording success for a long time, I went to see the manager of radio station

KFWB in Los Angeles. He was a Jewish gentleman, but he simply would not play my records.

I said, "Why won't you play my records?"

"Because they're an insult."

"What's insulting about them? All they are is harmless and well-meaning fun. You play all kinds of other comedy records. You play Mexican records."

"I don't play *any* ethnic records."

As we were talking, there came over the monitor of the man's own station Spike Jones' famous recording of "The Tennessee Waltz," with his girl singer giving it the "Ve vas valtzing, in de. . . ."

I said, "What about that one?"

"That's Spike Jones."

"What accent is his girl singer using?"

He said, "It does sound a little Jewish, doesn't it?"

But he still wouldn't play my records.

What *were* my records? As I've said, they were mostly English-Yiddish parodies of the top hits of the day. Over the years they have included:

> *Shleppin' (Walkin') My Baby Back Home*
> *Geshray of de Vilde Kotchke (Cry of the Wild Goose)*
> *Borscht Riders in the Sky*
> *Herring Boats Are Coming*
> *Dot's Morris*
> *(My version of Dean Martin's "That's Amore")*
> *Duvid Crockett*
> *Come Ona My Hois*
> *Feudin' and Fussin' with My Cousin*
> *The Little White Knish That Cried*
> *How Much Is That Pickle in the Window?*

And one of Walter Winchell's favorites:

> *KISS OF MEYER*
> *(Kiss of Fire)*
> *When I look on you,*

It burns by me a fire.
Come to Papa, bubele,
And have a kiss from Meyer . . .

And one of my warlike lyrics, without libretto or translation:

SOUND OFF
You're in de army, Schlaim,
Du bist nisht in der Haim;
You'll never get rich,
You old galitz,
You're in de army, Schlaim.
Sound off, sound off . . .
Mazel tov, mazel tov . . .
Sound off, mazel tov—
Heep hop—
Dot's all!

My "operas" include:

Carmen Katz
and
The Barber of Shlemiel.

Plus a great parody record of mine that I almost forgot: "It's a Treat to Beat Your Feet on the Mississippi Shmutz [Mud]."

And I don't want to miss mentioning some of my beautifully written (by others) instrumental recordings, which have included such numbers as:

Mannie Klein's "Mendel's Song"
Trombonist Si Zentner's "Trombonik Dance"
"Berele's Sherele" (a classic Yiddish melody) played by Benny Gill
"Haimish Memories" (Memories of Home)
And a great favorite of mine, "Grandma's Draidel" (a *draidel* is a "spinning top," a "turn" in a dance).

You will understand my frustration when radio station owners would not play these recordings.

I had a particularly infuriating experience in Philadelphia in the early days. When I was starring in one of my shows there, a musician friend of mine said that he used to enjoy hearing my records on a certain big Philadelphia radio station, but the station manager had recently taken them off the air. So I went to see him.

He was of our faith, but he looked up at me as much a stranger as a plate of lox at an Arab picnic. And you won't believe what happened next. He had an egg timer on his desk, and he ceremoniously "turned it over," wordlessly announcing to me that I had just three minutes of his valuable time. He said, "Mr. Katz, what can I do for you?"

I asked him why he wouldn't play my records. He said, "Because some of our listeners are offended."

I asked, "Who, besides you?"

He said, "I don't think that's any of your business."

I answered, "I think it is my business because this is how I make a living. You play Italian records, you play Polish records—"

He cut me off. "I will not play any record with Yiddish in it. Yiddish is the language of the ghetto."

His sand and my patience were rapidly running out.

"My friend," I said, "Yiddish is the language of our forefathers."

"I do not care to hear it."

"Then why don't you play some of my instrumental records? They're some of the greatest music in the world, played by some of the greatest musicians in the world— Ziggy Elman, Mannie Klein, Nat Farber—"

Again he cut me off in mid-sentence. "There will be no Yiddish spoken, and no Jewish music played, on this station."

My sand was gone. As I got up to leave, I told this miserable man, "Thank you very much. I think you're one of the most despicable anti-Semites I've ever had the misfortune to meet."

I met a similar situation when I recorded "Duvid Crockett." It was a tremendous hit—No. 2 on "the charts" all over the country. There was a two-page complimentary article in *Time* magazine about the recording. But the frightened Jewish editor of *Weekly Variety* took me to task for making a record that "defiled" the legend of Davy Crockett. The original Davy Crockett recording was itself a parody! The people knew this; they knew that I hadn't defiled anything; there was a sale of two hundred thousand on this recording. Here are some of the lyrics:

DUVID CROCKETT
Born in the wilds of Delancey Street,
Home of gefilte fish and kosher meat.
Handy wid a knife, O herzach tzi [listen to me],
He flicked him a chicken when he was only three.
Duvid, Duvid Crockett.
He sat in de sun and gerocket and gebocket [rocked back and forth].
Duvid, Duvid Crockett,
King of Delancey Street. . . .

My fans loved the record. But the frightened editor of *Weekly Variety* was not one of my fans.

But most of the Jewish people understood what I was doing. My records sold well all over the country, and Hal Zeiger almost immediately negotiated a better recording contract for me with Capitol, where I was to record for twenty years. I not only got a better royalty—five percent instead of RCA's two percent—but in addition, Capitol was a young, vigorous firm that did a great job of promoting its artists.

Aiding Hal in negotiating the new contract for me at Capitol was the fact that Alan Livingston, the young recording genius who headed Capitol, had originally come looking for me. He wanted me to impersonate a frog. He was doing a "Bozo the Clown" children's record, and for the frog sound, he was looking for "that guy who did the funny glug sounds on the Spike Jones' records." He found me, and I recorded Filbert the Frog (the frog who sings opera) for them.

My first album for Capitol—my first *album* for anyone—was a collection of my English-Yiddish "singles." It was called simply *Mickey Katz and His Orchestra*. Over the next fifteen years it sold more than one hundred thousand, which for a specialized album is a whale of a sale.

My second album for Capitol, and one that I love to this day, was also a big one. It was called *Mickey Katz Plays Music for Weddings, Bar Mitzvahs and Brisses*. (A *bris* is the circumcision ceremony.) The cover of this album is a delightful piece of artistic inspiration; it shows me, among other poses, sitting in a baby carriage, presumably after my own *bris,* smoking a cigar.

Other than the cover, this instrumental album had no comedy in it at all. If I do say so myself, it was simply delicious music. It was arranged by the late and great Nat Farber, who also played the piano in the orchestra for the album. Every note of the album breathes the flavor of the old but little-known *happy* Jewish music of the old country, yet all the tunes are original. It's simply wonderful, joyous but poignant music composed, arranged and played by a lot of extremely fine musicians.

Before I leave the story of my early recordings to go on to other things, there are a few people I want to remember to thank. First, I'll always be grateful to Walt Hebner and Eli Oberstein at RCA, who made my first record. And my heartfelt thanks to Alan Livingston and Voyle Gilmor of Capitol, who produced twenty of my biggest hit records.

Also, thanks to Steve Allen. He was one of the first of the Hollywood radio personalities to play my records on the air. I later appeared on Steve's network television show; he's still a very good friend.

And I'll never forget the *first* Hollywood personality to play my records over the air—Hawthorne, the funny guy with the oversized goggles. What a funny man! I don't know where he is today, but he was a big hit on Los Angeles radio, and deservedly so. I'll never forget how sad he was the day he called me up to tell me that he couldn't play my records anymore. He'd gotten a little flak from a few Jewish (!) listeners, and the station manager had demanded that he stop playing Mickey Katz records. This on one of the most hilarious comedy disc jockey shows in America!

It took television's *All in the Family* to kick the hell out of the frightened ones, and it took the Six-Day War in 1967, when a few thousand brave Jews in Israel proved to be more than a match for a hundred million Arabs, for "Jewish" finally to become popular and more acceptable.

But 1967 wasn't any help to me in *1947*, when I was working at Slapsie Maxie's, trying to do a funny English-Yiddish act and at the same time avoid Sy Devore, who was looking for me with a pink slip.

Fortunately at Slapsie Maxie's—as often happened with Slapsie Maxie himself in his own fighting days—I was saved by the bell. After the first week or two my records were being heard from coast to coast, and other stage offers were starting to come in by phone and telegram from all over the country, including Texas.

When Hal Zeiger looked over all these other offers and I asked him which one we should take next, his response was typical. He said, "If this many people want you, why work for any of them? Why work for some other asshole when you can work for yourself?"

8 · We Ring the Bell at the Wilshire Ebell— Papa and Son Joel

IT NEVER TOOK HAL ZEIGER long to make his move. He said, "Mick, let's produce an English-Yiddish stage revue."

I said, "I'm ready."

His next words were: "What shall we call this Yiddish hootenanny?"

Out of left field I answered, "How about calling it the *Borscht Capades?*"

Hal's enthusiasm was always instantaneous. He said, "Hey, that title's a winner! Line up some actors, and I'll get us a theater."

Which was more easily said than done. The two leading legitimate theaters in Los Angeles were the Philharmonic and the Biltmore, facing each other across Fifth Street downtown. But both of them booked only Broadway attractions that played a week or more. What we had in mind was renting a theater just for a night or two, for a tryout.

So Hal thought of the Wilshire Ebell. This was a professionally well-equipped theater with twelve hundred seats, owned by the illustrious Ebell Club, a group of prominent Los Angeles society ladies who rented out their theater for concerts and other cultural events. We wondered if "cultural events" would cover our English-Yiddish revue.

Fortunately the gentile gentleman who managed the Wilshire Ebell, Hal Pettijohn, agreed to rent it to us for one weekend. At that time, October 1948, there were only some two hundred and fifty thousand Jewish people in all of Southern California, but the Wilshire Ebell was a very handy location for all of them. The theater was in the prestigious Wilshire area just west of downtown. It was only two miles from the heavily Jewish section of Fairfax Avenue, five miles from Beverly Hills and the Jewish community around Pico and Robertson, and a fairly simple bus ride for the people from over east in Boyle Heights. Hal's getting the Wilshire Ebell was a great stroke of good judgment.

As Hal's province was handling the business arrangements, it was my responsibility to produce and cast the show. What I wanted to create was a high type of presentation that would appeal to all generations of the Jewish community.

The old Yiddish theater flourished in America for more than eighty years. The shows, done in a majestic manner and all in Yiddish, reflected the tragedy, the comedy and pathos of the Eastern European *shtetlach*. The Yiddish theater presented old Yiddish plays and original shows by such creative geniuses as Abe Ellstein and Joseph Rumshinsky, who wrote original and great music to some of the old country tales. The Yiddish theater was great theater, if you had a fluent knowledge of the language—which fewer and fewer people did.

As a youngster growing up in Cleveland I attended the Yiddish production at the Duchess Theater with my father and mother. My mother would cry through the whole show. My father would make small hisses at the villains. If a young actor in the play was being mean to his parents or grandparents, people in the audience would say aloud, "Shame on you!"

Many great American screen stars had their start in the Yiddish theater—Luther Adler, Paul Muni, and, on the contemporary scene, Herschel Bernardi and Leo Fuchs. "Bei Mir Bist Du Schoen," the Andrews Sisters' great hit record, came originally from the Yiddish theater.

But by 1948 the Yiddish theater had lost a great part of its audience. There simply weren't that many people anymore with a fluent knowledge of Yiddish. I felt in my heart that those in my generation would enjoy a new type of American Yiddish theater, done in Yiddish *and* English, with some of the talented young Catskills performers doing the comedy mostly in English and our vocalists singing the nostalgic and familiar folk songs of our people.

Speaking of the Catskills reminds me of the old couple who were snowed in one winter during a blizzard at their little home in the Jewish Alps. They were buried under the snow for three days—the whole little house and yard one vast ball of snow. Finally, the rescuers fought their way through to them with snow plows and bulldozers; they cleared the snow away enough to ring the doorbell, not knowing if anyone within was alive or dead. On the second ring of the doorbell the old man inside opened the door and said, "Who you?"

The rescuer joyfully announced, "We're from the Red Cross!"

The old man said, "We gave already."

For the *Borscht Capades* I assembled a cast of talented young American Jewish singers and comedians. Today many of them are big names in show business. But in 1948, since my recordings were already popular, Hal Zeiger cast me as headliner and master of ceremonies.

Then I selected the rest of the cast. First I hired comedian Phil Foster (who had gotten the ice cream and doughnuts for us on the USO tour). Phil fractured the audience with his routine about his mother and father and his boyhood in Brooklyn when he hung around the corner candy store.

For more comedy, I hired a young comedian named Rickie Layne, with his puppet, Velvel. Believe me, Velvel is a puppet and no dummy; he did some great Jewish shtiks.

I also presented Jackie Hilliard, a handsome young man who sang romantic English-Yiddish love songs; and lovely Raasche, who sang the bittersweet folk songs of our people in Yiddish.

In addition, I had a great six-piece band, including such legendary musicians as Mannie Klein and Ziggy Elman, playing our specially arranged "Jewish jazz." I played solo clarinet with them, and we gave the audience a lot of happy *frailachs*. In that original *Borscht Capades* I had all this.

But most of all, I had my son Joel.

In 1948 Joel was a sixteen-year-old boy attending Hamilton High School in Los Angeles. But he was already a pro in show business. His acting career had started at the age of eight.

My wife, Grace, had always had a love of theatrics. As a little girl she used to emote tear-jerking dramatic recitals, while her mother listened and proudly cried her eyes out. One of Grace's most effective renditions was about a little urchin boy named Tony, who was at the drugstore without any money, pleading for medicine for his sick mother. Grace's recital of "Tony" would have wrung tears out of the Internal Revenue Service.

So when Grace recognized a flair for acting in young Joel, she knew that here was destiny; here was the fruition of all her dreams. When she found out that she could enroll him in the children's theater at the Cleveland Play-house—the renowned Curtain Pullers—she clapped Joel's little tassel cap on him, and off they went.

Grace's dream of Joel's acting talent proved correct. Almost immediately he started getting parts in the Curtain Pullers' plays. One of his first roles was in *Hurricane Island*, in which he played a pathetic little storm-tossed refugee with a knapsack over his shoulder.

The dramatic teacher of the Curtain Pullers was Esther

Mullins. She was a delighted and devoted inspiration to the children. It was Esther who really started training Joel in show business. She once told Grace and me about Joel, "This boy is incredible. He has a flair for the dramatic that is out of this world."

Then came Joel's first "big break." K. Elmo Lowe, the director of the Cleveland Playhouse, was looking for a child to play the demanding role of Pud in its production of *On Borrowed Time*—Paul Osborn's dramatization of Lawrence E. Watkin's novel—in which nobody in the world can die till Death comes down out of the apple tree. The whole play revolves around little Pud and his grandfather, the latter role later played in the movie by Lionel Barrymore.

Joel happened to come by at just the right time. In Earl Wilson's column, Joel told about it better than anyone else could. He said, "Mr. Lowe spotted me on the way to the theater one day. I was wearing a big mackinaw and a big fur hat. I was nine at the time and barely above the ground in height."

Another columnist, Stan Anderson of the Cleveland *Press,* adds about the incident: "Since Joel as a child had an unusual dignity, in his over-sized garb he must have looked pretty amusing. Director Lowe, first telling Joel to stand right where he was, ran and called his wife, Dorothy Paxton. He said, 'Come out here and look at this—you won't believe it.' "

Joel got the coveted part of Pud in *On Borrowed Time.*

And in this demanding role, in the big theater, he was a sensation. He became a "star" overnight, at an age when most boys were learning to play marbles. It was, of course, too early for such adulation to come to any youngster. One night Joel showed the only fit of childish temperament I've ever known him to display. Forty-five minutes before curtain time, with a capacity audience already streaming into the theater, Joel suddenly announced backstage that he wouldn't go on unless his little cousin Burton was backstage with him. His little cousin Burton—now Lee Zuckerman of NBC—was across town in bed, asleep. But nothing would sway Joel; he remained calmly adamant. I finally rushed across town and brought little sleepy-eyed Burton to the theater—and Joel went on and did an outstanding performance.

(Joel never forgot his early days at the Cleveland Playhouse. Four years ago he went back and did a benefit for it in the big Cleveland Auditorium.)

Joel's success in *On Borrowed Time* led immediately to more roles in the adult playhouse. In *Family Portrait,* the life of Christ, Joel played a cousin of Jesus. I'll never forget the night we took my father to see Joel in this play. He looked at his grandson up on the stage with Jesus, and then he looked at us. His look said, "What kind of play is this for a Jewish boy?"

At any rate, Joel, while still a very small boy, was the talk of the town. All our friends told Grace and me that we must take him to New York at once—and throw him into the Broadway cement mixer.

We didn't, and I'm glad that we didn't. As nearly as possible Joel enjoyed a normal boyhood. I wanted him to grow up as a happy youngster and then an aspiring actor. That's the way it worked out, and I'm glad that it did.

But when I told Joel that I was going to produce the *Borscht Capades,* he smelled the Promised Land. He said, "Dad, I want to be in your show."

Without thinking, I said, "What can you do in this show? It's an English-Yiddish show. You can't speak Yiddish."

Two days later Joel came to me and said, "I can sing 'Rumania, Rumania' in your show."

All by himself, he had picked out a real rouser of a song. He'd found it on a record by the great eighty-four-year-old actor from the Yiddish theater Aaron Lebedeff. It was a song about the early life in Rumania and all the Rumanian goodies, the little pastramis that were so delicious, and the great Rumanian wine, and the baklava and the other wonderful native delicacies.

The number was sung all in Yiddish! The only Yiddish
Joel knew was from hearing his grandparents speak it
around the house. But when he sang "Rumania, Rumania"
for me, his Yiddish was perfect! He'd played the record
over and over, rehearsed it a hundred times. Joel still does
"Rumania, Rumania" in his act today.

When Joel first did the number for me, his rendition was
so sensational I could hardly sit still. I told Hal to put him
in the show.

Here's how I presented Joel in the *Borscht Capades:*

I put him on in the second half of the show. The audience
didn't know that he was my son. We billed him as Joel
Kaye. As part of my act in the first half I did my record
rendition of "Tico, Tico." Joel came on in the second
half, did an opening number and then his great number,
"Rumania, Rumania," and when the applause wouldn't
stop, he would come back out for an encore. For his encore,
he proceeded to do "Tico, Tico" *exactly* as I had done it
in the first half! In the middle of the number I came hesi-
tantly back onstage, a hand to my face in feigned surprise
and unhappiness as I watched this young upstart stealing
my act! I gradually joined in dancing and singing with
Joel on the number, and we ended up both doing my glugs
and my other comedy shtiks, Joel matching me every step
of the way. When we finished, the applause was like an
explosion.

Then all I had to do was to smile at the audience and tell
them that he was my son—and the whole place went crazy.
The heartwarming family love of our audience made the
number an unforgettable smash.

(From that first *Borscht Capades* on Joel became everybody's son. He's now forty-four and an international headliner, yet when my fans greet me anywhere in America,
they ask, "How's the kid?")

When Joel opened with us in the *Borscht Capades* at the
Wilshire Ebell, he'd never had a dancing lesson in his life,

yet he danced like a whirling dervish; he literally flew through the air. Our reviews were all raves, and Joel's press notices were superraves.

We sold out at the Wilshire Ebell every weekend for the next six months. We sold out so regularly that the good ladies of the Ebell Club, reading our steady flow of publicity in the press, began to have concern that we were turning their cultural Wilshire Ebell into a "Jewish" theater. So Hal and I invited their governing committee to come over and see the show. When they saw that our show was in good taste and attracted a family audience, they said we could continue. So what else? We continued.

After six months of capacity crowds at the Wilshire Ebell, Hal decided it was time to take the *Borscht Capades* on the road. He booked us for three weeks into the Eighth Street Theater in Chicago—on Wabash Avenue, part of the present site of the Hilton Hotel. The Eighth Street Theater was the only Chicago theater we could get at the time, the problem with it being that the famous *National Barn Dance* was broadcast from there every Saturday night. So we couldn't play Saturday night, which anywhere in the world is the biggest night in show business. Hal solved that situation by getting us two Saturday nights at the big Chicago Opera House (we sold that place out, too), and we played another sellout Saturday night in Milwaukee.

Hal had also worked hard at selling theater parties for the other nights of the week. Theater parties, in which charity fund raisers use an evening at the theater to raise money for a favorite charity, are of great importance to any new show. They were of crucial importance to our show because charity-inclined Jewish ladies are always raising money for *something*. Thank goodness, one of their favorite methods of raising money is to organize theater parties. And what more natural show for a Jewish theater party than the *Borscht Capades!*

The greatest city in America for theater parties is New

York because there the fund raisers pay full box-office price for the tickets; then they add on the 25 percent, 50 percent, or 100 percent or whatever differential they want to make for their charity. In most other cities around the country, the fund raisers want you to discount your tickets 25 percent to a third; then they sell the tickets at the box-office price or more for their charity causes. This can incidentally create "nervous time" because when they sign the contract, you often get only a deposit, and then you pray that you'll get the balance before show time. Fortunately you usually do—fortunately because it's not very nice to sue a synagogue or a hospital for unsold tickets!

After New York the second-best city in the country for theater parties is Chicago. I remember one time when we were opening a new *Borscht Capades* show in Chicago and Hal was talking simultaneously to four different women from four different fund-raising organizations. There was a lady from a temple, a lady from a B'nai B'rith auxiliary, a lady from a hospital, and another sweet lady from a sanitarium. And they all were knowledgeable business-women when it came to buying theater parties.

One would say, "Mr. Zeiger, how many seats are there in your theater?"

Hal answered that there were fourteen hundred.

"How are you scaling the house?"

"We're scaling the house from five dollars down to three dollars."

"How much do you want for the entire theater for Tuesday night, December the nineteenth?"

"Well, the crowds have been near capacity, and the way we're scaling the house the nightly gross is five thousand."

The woman wrote a check and handed it to him. "Here's a check for thirty-five hundred if we can have the whole house for the nineteenth."

A few of those Monday through Thursday, and you can take your chances on the other nights. Actually, we had standing-room-only crowds on the weekends, even the Sunday matinees. After our opening engagement at the Eighth Street Theater we later solved the Saturday night problem by an eight-week run at Chicago's prestigious Blackstone Theater, where we also did capacity business.

But all this financial talk is really of no importance in telling the story of that first year of the *Borscht Capades*. The important thing is the personal story of Joel and myself, a father and son traveling together on the road for the first time, as co-stars of a hit show. If this had ever happened before, I don't know of it. Certainly it is an unusual human experience.

When we decided to take the *Borscht Capades* on the road, Grace and I had to make some decisions about the family. Joel had by then graduated from high school and had enrolled at UCLA for long enough to convince him that he wanted to be in show business instead of a "profession," so he was free to travel with the show. But Ronnie, four years younger, at thirteen, was still in junior high. So at first Grace stayed in Los Angeles to take care of Ronnie while he went to school, and Joel and I went east with the *Borscht Capades*.

And let me tell you, it wasn't the easiest thing in the world, traveling with your son as co-stars of a hit show. I had thousands of fans from my records, and Joel's performances were so fantastic that he received almost daily raves in the papers. So our relationship rapidly changed from father and son to two starring actors—one aged forty and one aged seventeen.

It was a unique and in some ways a difficult situation. My idea of relaxing on the road was to get up early and take a nice walk. Joel, like all seventeen-year-old boys, wanted to stay up late so he wouldn't miss anything. So we each had our own hotel room, and after the show Joel went out on the town with Rickie Layne, Jackie Hilliard, and the other younger members of the cast. I went back to my hotel room. Joel loved me, but he was a teenager growing up—he didn't want to be tied down to his father. I tried to understand his feelings.

But some of those early-morning walks were damned lonely.

Another thing that contributed to my loneliness was a decision that Hal had talked me into before we left Los Angeles. I wanted to take some of my great musicians with me—Mannie Klein, Ziggy Elman—but Hal said, "Mick, forget it. We can't take a bunch of musicians to Chicago; it would cost us a fortune. They've got musicians in Chicago —quit worrying."

Which was, of course, good sense. I hired five musicians in Chicago, but they weren't *my* musicians. Without my musicians back of me on the stage, I felt naked.

After our first few weeks at the Blackstone Theater I developed a case of stage fright that would have destroyed Milton Berle.

My emotional problem—you will have to try to under-stand and believe this—was that I was suddenly too success-ful. The crowds packed the Blackstone to the rafters. There were nights when the scalpers sold tickets for $20 or $30, which is like a $100 ticket today.

To see *me!* Of course, to see Joel and the rest of the show, but when in torment, you tend to think of yourself. I began to think of the whole audience paying all that money to see little Mickey Katz walk out on that famous Blackstone stage that had held the Barrymores and Lunt and Fontanne. I began to feel so alone when it was time for me to walk out on that stage that it's impossible to describe.

And Joel and I hardly saw each other except when we were onstage. He was a starring actor in his own right and quite properly living his own life. I couldn't burden him with my problem. And Grace and Ronnie were back home in Los Angeles. . . .

After a few more weeks of keeping all this locked up

inside me, I got to the point where I thought that the next
time I walked out on that stage I'd die out there. I don't
mean that I thought that my act would die—*I* would die.
There were nights when I'd walk out on the stage and
almost completely black out. I'd "wake up" many minutes
later, maybe in the middle of my second or third number,
with hardly any memory of the numbers I'd already done.

It was, of course, simply my own version of stage fright.
Stage fright turns your blood to water and your bones to
Jell-o. It's sheer terror.

And I had no defense against it. I didn't drink—I never
have; one swallow of brandy, and I'm higher than a kite—
and I didn't take pills, "uppers" or "downers." I know
some famous comedians, very funny men, who wouldn't
think of walking out on a stage without first taking a
couple of belts of booze to drown the butterflies in their
stomachs. Certain concert artists throw up before going
out to play a concerto. That's why individual stars get a
lot of money—because they have to face audiences alone.
That's why a lot of stars need a bunch of freeloading
hangers-on to keep telling them they're great. Man, you're
the greatest, you got it made. . . .

At the Blackstone there was nobody to tell me anything.
And I felt increasingly like nothing. It got to the point
where I had to talk to somebody. So I went to see the house
doctor at the Congress Hotel where I was staying. As I look
back on those days, I can see that he was a pretty wise
doctor. After a thorough examination he said, "There's
nothing wrong with you. Nothing physical. Your trouble
isn't that you're afraid of dying—you're afraid of living."

When Hal got wind of what was going on, he gave me
the same advice in a different way. He said, "Mick, if you
don't want to be a star, just go home and stay in bed. Nobody will bother you there. But if you do want to be a star,
stop the horseshit and get out there and do the show."

So I went out and did the show. And I got steadily more

depressed and ill. I was a sick Hebrew; I was a psychotic smash. I knew that the time was rapidly approaching when I could no longer keep forcing myself to perform.

Then early one morning, after a nightmarish sleepless night, there was a knock on my hotel room door. I opened it, and there stood Grace! She'd evidently just got off a plane from Los Angeles. She said, "I heard you weren't feeling well." I pulled her into the room, put my arms around her, and all the panic and misery went away.

After the Blackstone we played Minneapolis, Toronto, Montreal. . . . When we got off the train at Montreal, all I could see was snow. It was a blizzard like I never saw in my life. And I came from Cleveland, the home of blizzards. But this blizzard made Cleveland seem like the Caribbean. After I got settled in at the hotel (with Grace!), I put on a big overcoat and galoshes and went mushing off to His Majesty's Theater to see if we should try to put on a show.

I mushed for five blocks through two feet of snow, which was getting deeper. I was gradually disappearing into it. When I got within sight of the theater, I couldn't believe my eyes. Dimly through the snow, I could see a long queue of customers waiting at the box office.

That night they turned out to be possibly the most wonderful audience of our whole tour. While the blizzard raged outside, we gradually got thawed out up on the stage, and for three hours we all had a ball. I don't know whether to call it a matzo ball or a snowball.

Then, in January 1950, we took the *Borscht Capades* to Florida—to Miami Beach.

When I first had gone down there, in 1937—Grace and I drove down just for the trip—Miami Beach had only a few hotels catering to a Jewish clientele, and they were jammed into a small area called South Beach.

That reminds me of a joke. By 1951 all the beautiful new hotels—the Fontainebleau, the Eden Roc, the Saxony—had been built on upper Collins Avenue, but some of the older people, with limited funds, still went to South Beach.

Occasionally they would walk the sixteen blocks from Lincoln Road up to the lordly reaches of upper Collins Avenue, to see what was going on among the jet set.

One morning two of these elderly ladies from South Beach were walking up Collins Avenue when one of them stopped. She said to her friend, "Just a minute, I've got to stop and rest. I'm having such hot flushes I could die."

Her friend said, "Hot flushes? Tell me, dahling, have you been through the menopause?"

The other old lady said, "To tell you the truth, I haven't even been through the Fontainebleau."

I love these stories about our beloved Yiddish mamas, with their beautiful humor and their wonderful expressions. Do you remember Mr. Anthony in the old radio days? He'd go through the audience with his microphone, asking people about their problems.

On one of his programs he stopped beside a little lady who seemed terribly distraught. He said, "And what can I do for you, dear? Do you have a problem?"

The little woman started crying. Through her tears she said, "Nobody can help me with my problem. I'm married for thirty-three years, and yesterday Sam came home and told me he wants a divorce. Tomorrow night at five o'clock he's bringing home the *lawyer!*"

Mr. Anthony said, "I'm sorry to hear that, but what is your question?"

"My question is: Do I have to cook supper for the lawyer, too?"

Then there's the pair of sweet old ladies in the Catskills, sitting in their rocking chairs in their *kochalayn* (cook alone). A *kochalayn* is a little separate cottage with its own cooking facilities; many of the older Catskills hotels had these little cottages where people who didn't have much money could stay on a vacation. The only trouble with a *kochalayn* was that there wasn't much social life, meaning none. These two lovely little old ladies had been cooped up in their *kochalayn* for nearly a week; they were completely talked out and trying desperately to think of something to say.

Finally, one said, "Tell me, dahling, what would you do if you found a million dollars?"

The other old lady thought this question over carefully, then said, "Well, if a poor person lost it, I would give it back."

Let me tell you one more grandma story. When comedian Larry Best was just starting out in the Catskills, he played a little hotel auditorium that was so small the audience was practically sitting in his lap. Larry was a new performer, and while telling his jokes, he was greatly encouraged by one elderly lady in the first row, who kept saying, "Goot, goot, ay goot."

When he finished and had time to find this lady out in the lobby to thank her, he walked up to her, put his arms around her, and said, "Sweetheart, I'm so glad that you liked my act!"

She looked at him blankly and said, "Who you?"

"Why, I'm the actor you just enjoyed so much. All during my act you kept saying, 'Goot, goot.' "

"Oh, dot. I've got arthritis in my shoulder, and your spotlight was baking me in de back, so I said, 'Goot, goot, ay goot!' "

When we arrived in Miami Beach in January 1950 to play the *Borscht Capades,* the South Beach ghetto had been broken. Beautiful new hotels were being built by eastern investors all over upper Collins Avenue, all the way up to Forty-fifth Street. But there were only movie theaters, nothing suitable for a stage revue. There was a theater down in South Beach, on lower Washington Avenue, that played occasional Yiddish shows, but neither Hal nor I wanted to go that route with the *Borscht Capades.*

So Hal got an idea. There was a beautiful little thousand-seat movie theater—the Roosevelt on Forty-first Street, near the Eden Roc and the other newer hotels—but it didn't have a stage. Not to be daunted by a little detail like no stage, Hal rented the Roosevelt and spent $4000 having a stage built so we could play the *Borscht Capades* there.

When the *Borscht Capades* opened at the Roosevelt, the Miami and Miami Beach newspapers all gave the show rave reviews, and we were suddenly the hit of the town. In those days Miami Beach was the "in" place to go. The new crowd was an elegant crowd of people of means and position. When we were playing the Roosevelt, you could look out from the stage any night and see in the audience one of the Warner brothers, Colonel Jake Arvey, the Democratic national committeeman from Chicago, David Dubinsky, the famous head of the International Ladies Garment Workers Union. . . .

Miami Beach had never presented a top-level American Jewish show, and it welcomed our humor, and our happy *frailach* music, with open arms. The lines at the box office every day looked like a sale at Macy's.

And the Katz family had a wonderful time. We'd all come to Miami from the West Coast together, Joel and I and Grace and Ronnie. We rented a big penthouse at my good friend Chuckie Goldberg's beautiful Delano Hotel right on the beach at seventeenth and Collins (are you ready for this—in 1950 our Miami Beach penthouse cost $35 per day!). The show was doing capacity business, our family was together in love and comfort. . . .

Evidently we were having too much pleasure. The bubble was about to break.

We discovered that the owners of the Roosevelt Theater were about to give us a bad time. They operated a big chain of movie theaters in New York City. During our six-week engagement at their Roosevelt in Miami Beach they had been looking at the lines at our box office with great interest. When it came time to talk about renewing our rental option, they refused to renew it unless we gave them a higher percentage of the gross, plus agreed to move the show later into one of their New York theaters.

Well, you know what Hal Zeiger said to that. He said, "Up your clyde, gentlemen." He said it so loud that people heard him in Key West. He told them that we didn't need them to take our show to New York.

Hal was a fighter. But this time he was fighting City Hall.

Because in addition to that situation, another important event occurred—Mr. Eddie Cantor. Let me hasten to add that if it hadn't been Eddie Cantor, some other producer would have inevitably appeared on the scene to "discover" my son and give him the opportunity to move on and grow.

At that point in our lives Eddie Cantor and Jennie Grossinger came to the Roosevelt one night to see the show. Hal and I met them after the show, Joel was introduced to them, and Cantor told Hal and me that he would like to engage Joel for his forthcoming television *Colgate Comedy Hour*.

Hal said to me, "What do you think about Cantor taking Joel out of the show?"

I said, "Look, Hal, this is Joel's big chance; I'm for it all the way. Joel has his own life to live, and I want him to live it."

So Joel played the last two weeks of our engagement at the Roosevelt; then he left for the Coast to join Eddie Cantor. (As I recall, it was while working with a writer on new material for the *Colgate Comedy Hour* that Joel changed his stage name to Joel Grey.)

In the meantime, Hal decided to take the *Borscht Capades* into New York.

When we left the Roosevelt because of the unacceptable terms, little did we know what mischief lurked in the minds of the theater operators. Before we left the Roosevelt, they —with the help of a couple of Catskills booking agents named Beckman and Pransky—put together a cheaper version of the *Borscht Capades,* called it *Bagels and Yocks,* and put it into their Miami Beach theater. On our $4000 stage! Legally, there was nothing we could do about it. They ran their show successfully for eight more weeks, clear up to May 15, a month after the normal close of the top Miami Beach tourist season.

At the same time Hal was in New York, selling theater parties and getting ready to open the *Borscht Capades* on Broadway in the fall. Never let it be said that he didn't go first class. He leased the Shubert Royale Theater, on Forty-fifth Street between Broadway and Eighth Avenue, right in the middle of the top Broadway legitimate theater area. He started hiring people right and left, including a line of beautiful girls to be a kosher version of the Rockettes (one of the dancers in our chorus line was present star Carol Lawrence). Hal even paid cartoonist Al Capp $5,000 to paint us a wonderful curtain, showing a delightful little man sitting at a table eating a bowl of borscht.

During this time I was getting a *Borscht Capades* cast ready for Broadway, including Phil Foster, Dave Barry, the Barry Sisters—with special music written for us by Joseph Rumshinsky of New York Yiddish theater fame. We got a beautiful show together.

And a week before we were to open, the Brandts opened their *Bagels and Yocks* in one of their theaters two blocks up the street! To some of the worst reviews you've ever read in your life! The New York dramatic press didn't want *any* English-Yiddish show on Broadway; Yiddish shows were supposed to be presented on the Lower East Side or over in Brooklyn. Certainly not on Broadway. So the critics took advantage of the opportunity to clobber *Bagels and Yocks* with hobnailed typewriters. They said the show set race relations back a hundred years. And then they got less complimentary.

In truth, *Bagels and Yocks* wasn't that bad. It was a frank copy of our format, and like most copies, it wasn't anywhere near as good as the original; but it wasn't all that terrible. They had talented performers in their cast but there were decided differences in the quality and name value of the production. For instance, since their theater—the Holiday at Forty-seventh and Broadway—was classified as a movie theater instead of being in the actual legitimate theater area, the Musicians Union gave them permission to use only eight men in their orchestra, whereas we were compelled to use *eighteen*.

Possibly because of quality differences like that, when we opened the *Borscht Capades* a week later, the critics were kinder to us. The *Daily News* said, "Mickey Katz, well-known for his Capitol records, is also listed as co-producer of the show, and he earned his title." The *Tribune*, on the other hand, sent a "society-type" critic, who headlined his review *Borscht Sour*.

But the New York *Times* review was most heartening, calling the *Borscht Capades* "a show made up of great talents and great music." The *Times* complimented some of our "talented people," particularly Phil Foster. And they were highly complimentary about the music written for us by Joseph Rumshinsky, who was, of course, well known to them from his great work in the New York Yiddish theater.

So our press notices, under the circumstances, really weren't bad. Incidentally, here are my feelings about critics' reviews. When you open a show, if you get a good review, it helps you, slightly; a fair review, you're on your way to the poorhouse; a really bad review, you're on your way to the outhouse; a *rave* review, forget everything I've said up to now, you're on your way to being the Jewish P. T. Barnum.

But basically, it wasn't the reviews—either ours or *Bagels'*—that killed us. It was just the intolerable situation where, for the first time, there was a direct confrontation between two English-Yiddish shows running simultaneously within two blocks of each other. Even in New York City there just wasn't that much business for two specialized shows of this type. If we could have taken the *Borscht Capades* into New York without the competition of the Brandts, we'd have easily made half a million dollars.

In the meantime, Joel was out in Hollywood and had completed his eight weeks on the *Colgate Comedy Hour* with Eddie Cantor, to great reviews. Syndicated columnist Harriet Van Horne said, "Joel Grey, charged with furious energy, sang and danced marvelously. . . ."

Joel had also appeared in his first movie, *About Face,* for Warner Brothers. *Daily Variety* said of this very first movie of Joel's: "Joel Grey handles his comedy well and socks over his one number in fine style."

Toward the end of our New York run Joel, his movie completed and wanting to do anything he could to help, came back to New York and rejoined the *Borscht Capades.* But it was too late for even that to help—with *Bagels and Yocks* still two blocks up the street self-destructing us both.

As our New York adventure went gurgling down the drain, a tender family moment occurred. As business continued to get worse, Hal Zeiger called a meeting of the cast and asked everybody to take a 20 percent cut.

In the middle of the cast was my son. He was also a known professional actor. (He was still only eighteen!) In the meeting with him were his fellow actors, who felt they shouldn't take a cut. They were doing their job and doing a good job; they didn't feel that they should take a cut just because we were losing money. They were all experienced nightclub performers, most of whom could go to work some place else the next day. Why should they suffer along with us? They had their own careers to worry about.

When Joel found out the tone of the meeting, he told the other members of the cast, "I'm an actor—I have a strong feeling for what you're doing. But I also have a very strong feeling for my father. You're going to have to hold this meeting without me. I pass." And he walked away. I saw Joel later that afternoon, and I know how unhappy he was.

At any rate, after four months of "Slaughterhouse Near

Eighth Avenue," bucking *Bagels and Yocks,* I gave up. Hal wanted to move the show to a larger theater on Broadway, where we could maybe cut the price of the tickets and start something new. But I'd had enough. I said, "Hal, we tried, we lost, we're busted. I don't want any more." We'd lost $70,000—$35,000 apiece—which was all I had. I'd sent Grace and Ronnie back to the Coast a week earlier. Joel stayed on in New York, and I took a plane for Los Angeles.

We still had the little house I'd bought on Malcolm Avenue in West Los Angeles. I'd bought it for $13,500 when I was with Spike Jones. We could live there till I could get into action again.

Shortly after I arrived home, I received a call from a gentleman with the Internal Revenue Service. After a final check on the tax situation from our New York production, the IRS determined that we owed an additional tax bite of $5500. Since I had been a partner, my half was $2750—which I didn't have. Hal had paid his half. When might the government expect my check? To make sure that it would get my check, the IRS had put a lien on my house.

But if I owed the government anything, I wanted to pay it, lien or no lien. I sold the house at a loss—for $11,500, a loss of $2000—and I paid the IRS. Then with hardly anything left out of the equity in the house, Grace and Ronnie and I moved into an apartment.

Soon after we moved into the apartment, I got a letter from Joel from New York. Through the William Morris Agency he'd signed a contract with ABC, he'd just received his first check, and he enclosed a check to me for $1000.

I said, "Grace, look at this." And I cried.

Because even though we were three thousand miles apart, our family was together again.

9 · Of Dice and Men— Also Broads... Next Stop-Las Vegas!

THE *Borscht Capades* New York disaster was a killer. I arrived home broke, but not bent. For several weeks I pondered what fate might still have in store for Mickey Katz.

And one morning I found out. A Los Angeles packager of radio programs called me and asked how I'd like to be a kosher disc jockey.

I said, "What else?"

He said that the exposure would be terrific. After our frenzied adventures in New York what I needed at this time was not *exposure,* but composure. But half a bagel is better than nottin', so I accepted the deal.

And from 1951 to 1956, I was Southern California's only American Jewish disc jockey. I did the commentaries and commercials in English-Yiddish comic vein, as I'd done the *Borscht Capades.* The station manager of ABC's big Los Angeles radio station, KABC, was a wonderful gentleman named Amos Baron. He wasn't afraid to put on a "Jewish" radio show. He said, "Let's try it for two weeks, and see what happens." He gave me an hour on his station for two Sunday evenings from five to six o'clock—and I was on for five years.

I did my talking mostly in English, but my program featured recordings with a Yiddish-Israeli flavor. I played Al Jolson's great Yiddish recordings. I also played Jolson's great record in English of "The Anniversary Waltz," which had started out in the old country as a Yiddish waltz.

Jewish mamas and papas have always loved waltzes. There's a wonderful story about the old couple who were dancing in Miami Beach. In the old days all the hotels there had "dancing classes." And since it was Florida, the dancing classes usually featured Latin music. Well, one day our elderly couple were dancing to Pupi Campo's band at one of the hotels, and Sam, trying to keep up with the lively Latin rhythm, was stepping all over his wife's feet. Finally, she said, "Waltz a little faster, Sam; they're playing a fox-trot."

On my program I also played the Yiddish recordings of Jan Peerce and Richard Tucker, the great opera stars who also made cantorial recordings. I played records from Europe and Israel, including those of the great Dutch singing star Leo Fuld, among them his heartbreaking recording called "Where Can I Go?" about a poor soul who had lived through a Nazi concentration camp and who now wondered what was next going to happen to him.

Even the Irish joined the act! Dennis Day made one great English-Yiddish record called "Shluf, Mein Kind [Sleep, My Child]." He did a first chorus in English, then a second chorus in Yiddish. Connie Stevens, who is an Italian-American, recorded a whole album in Yiddish of great Jewish folk songs. One of the best instrumental recordings was by Gordon Jenkins, who made a fine album of all the great Jewish folk music, done symphonic style.

I also, of course, played all my own English-Yiddish recordings. I was one disc jockey who wasn't afraid to play them! I also featured the records of the two great female Israeli stars Shoshana Damari and Yaffa Yarkoni and, of course, many of the wonderful Israeli recordings celebrating Israel's 1948 independence.

I must mention one other album that was a big hit on

the show, as well as in record stores all over America. In 1953 I suggested to Joel that he make a Yiddish album with my band. We would call it "Songs My Father Taught Me." Joel made the album, all in Yiddish—fourteen popular Yiddish folk songs. Again, Joel's perfect Yiddish just knocked me out. You'd have thought he'd spent many years performing in the Yiddish theater on Second Avenue in New York. His Yiddish *gefiel* (feeling) and vocal expression were filled with the deepest spirit of *Yiddishkeit*.

I had many guest stars on my show—Joel, George Jessel, Sophie Tucker, Sam Levenson, Tennessee Ernie Ford, Guy Mitchell, and Maurice Schwartz, the great dramatic star of the Yiddish theater, plus, of course, the civic and religious leaders of the community on the Jewish holidays.

I had two sponsors who stayed with me the whole five years: the Desert Inn in Las Vegas and Canter's famous delicatessen and restaurant on Fairfax Avenue. Such loyalty! My other sponsors included Manischewitz Wine, Mother's Gefulte Fish, and Pepsi-Cola. Pepsi-Cola?

The greatest personal satisfaction I got from my radio show was its wide appeal. Thousands of people of all faiths loved the *haimish* (homey) Jewish music and the lively *frailachs*. I got grateful letters from Catholic senior citizens and from many non-Jewish individuals and groups.

There were many people in the Hollywood motion-picture community who loved the show—Edward G. Robinson, Sam Jaffe, Ray Bolger. . . . One show-business incident in particular was a great pleasure to me. Grace and I were having dinner one night at the Luau in Beverly Hills when George Burns and Gracie Allen and Jack Benny and Mary Livingstone walked in. I knew George and Benny from the Friars. George asked me to come over to their table so he could introduce me to Gracie and Mary. He said, "Gracie, you know that program you listen to every Sunday night? This is Mickey Katz." Gracie said, "Mickey, I love your show." At this praise coming from such a sweet and wonderful lady, I was thrilled.

In addition to the radio show from 1951 to 1956 and between more road tours with Hal Zeiger, I played several four- to six-week engagements at Billy Gray's famous Bandbox nightclub at Beverly and Fairfax, in the center of the Los Angeles Jewish community. Billy Gray in my opinion is one of the greatest Jewish comics of all time. His cherubic little face and manner convulsed the audiences. Around 1953 Sammy Lewis, who had owned and managed the original Slapsie Maxie's, became a partner with Billy Gray in the Bandbox, and they put on some of the most hilarious parodies of "book shows" that I have ever seen. The shows were written by Sid Kuller, and they were *funny*—among them, "My Fairfax Lady" and "The Cohen Mutiny." Co-starring with Billy Gray in these shows were fabulous Patty Moore and Ben Lessy.

This was the time when television was just starting, and all the big eastern comics who were coming out to break into television played Billy Gray's Bandbox—Joey Bishop, Buddy Hackett, Phil Foster. . . .

Being a dutiful son, Billy Gray moved his mother out from the icy climate of Omaha. He set her up in a nice little apartment in Ocean Park, which at that time was a beach retirement place for elderly Jewish people, a sort of Coney Island West.

After getting settled in her apartment, Billy's mother asked him if he could help her join a nice synagogue. Billy had helped raise money for a little Orthodox synagogue not far from where his mother lived, and he took her over there and introduced her to the ladies of the congregation. He said, "Ladies, this is my mother, Mrs. Geventer, and she would like to become a member of the *shul.*"

The president of the sisterhood immediately responded, "Make her a member? We will make her an officer!" And with a great burst of applause, the ladies proceeded to elect Billy Gray's mother recording secretary.

The only trouble was that this honor went to her head, as was evident at the next meeting of the sisterhood two weeks hence. After a few items of routine business the president announced, "And now, I think we should hear a couple words from our new recording secretary." Everyone waited with bated breath to hear the maiden speech from the mother of this famous comedian.

They did not know Mrs. Geventer. She was a lady of many years, but with lots of *chutzpa*. She rose and said, "Vell, first I don't think that we ladies should sit upstairs and the boys sit downstairs; I think we should mingle. And I don't think we should have an old rabbi like the one we got it. I think we should have a young modern rabbi about age twenty-five."

Not realizing that her audience was stirring with something other than pleasure, she went on blithely, "And foider, I think our cantor should sing more a glee club style, a little more like a Sinatra. . . ."

She finally quit talking and sat down to thunderous silence. Then the president rose and faced her. "Mrs. Geventer," she said, "we clapped you in; we'll clap you out."

Also during this time Hal Zeiger and I took the *Borscht Capades* on many tours. We played Boston, where we were a smash. We even took the *Borscht Capades* to Texas—to El Paso, San Antonio, Houston and Dallas. In El Paso a man came up to the bandstand and said to me, "You Jew?"

I said, "What did you say?"

He repeated it: "You Jew?"

I said, "What about it? You want to fight?"

He said, "Who wants to fight? We need you for a *minyan!*"

Also in El Paso, Ziggy Elman led a band of Mexican-American musicians for the show who not only didn't dig Yiddish, but didn't dig English! Not a word. Even with Ziggy doing his best, our *frailachs* sounded like cha-cha-chas.

Next we went to Pittsburgh, where Hal had booked us into the Syria Mosque, the big Masonic temple there.

And as usual with me, a funny thing happened on the way to the mosque. As you may remember, my fine conductor friend Maurice Spitalny had left Cleveland to become musical head of the big Pittsburgh radio station, KDKA. Well, Maurice was still there, in all his glory. Hal had already engaged him to act as our "contractor" in hiring the local musicians for our orchestra. I also thought that since Maurice was a big wheel in radio, he might be the means of getting my Los Angeles radio show syndicated into Pittsburgh and the East Coast. I'd made a transcription of the show, and when I called Maurice from Los Angeles to broach the subject of syndication, he said, "Kid, you bring the record. I'll play it for the bosses."

When I got to Pittsburgh, Maurice, true to his word, had arranged an audition, with a control room full of important-looking gentlemen. Being Maurice, he did it his own way. He'd play a few bars of the transcription, then stop for comments. For instance, during the part that sampled some of my guest stars, Sophie Tucker's famous throaty voice came on. Maurice, pretending that he didn't recognize her voice, stopped the record and said, "Mickey, who's that?"

When I said it was Sophie Tucker, Maurice turned to the others with a big winning smile and said, "That was Sophie Tucker! This kid knows everybody!"

He proceeded through the whole transcription this way, stopping the record every minute or so to impress the others with my Hollywood magnificence. But finally, a voice came on the transcription that he'd really never heard before. He said, "Mickey, who is that fellow?"

I said, "That's Billy Gray."

It didn't stop Maurice. He turned to the others and said, "How do you like that? He's even got Billy Graham on his program!"

Maurice didn't sell the radio show for me, but it was nice seeing him again.

During 1952 I had another interesting experience. I took out a little four-piece band and did some shows for the United Jewish Appeal. The dates were booked out of the United Jewish Appeal office in Los Angeles. I was paid $500 for each date, which meant that after paying four musicians, I wasn't getting rich; but the dates were fun, and the audiences were great. I played places like Phoenix, Tucson, Portland, San Jose.

One night at Salinas, in the lettuce country eighty miles south of San Francisco, the audience in the synagogue kept asking me not to start the show yet because they were waiting for a rich old rancher named Lefcourt.

And Mr. Lefcourt was not appearing. The committee knew that he'd want to see the show, but *he* knew that he was going to be tapped for a sizable pledge, so everybody knew that he would try to slip into the synagogue after the show was under way.

Well, I didn't want to hold the start of the performance past nine o'clock, so when it got well past eight-thirty, I asked the committee what Mr. Lefcourt looked like. They said he was a stubby little man who always wore cowboy boots and a big Stetson hat. I went out and stood in front of the synagogue, and in a few minutes here came a man who had to be Lefcourt. He sidled up to me and said quietly, "Is de show started yet?"

I told him that it was just about to start. His next question was: "Mickey Katz—he's here?" I assured him that Mickey Katz was here and was just about to start the show. So Mr. Lefcourt carefully walked into the synagogue.

As he entered, the whole audience jumped up and cried, "Welcome, Mr. Lefcourt! We wouldn't start the show without you. And thank you for your pledge!"

Mr. Lefcourt was caught with his chaps down, and he pledged $500.

And then came Las Vegas.

Hal Zeiger and I had toured a new edition of the *Borscht Capades* called *The Farfel Follies,* and when we got back home in 1953, I decided it was time for me to play Las Vegas since musical lounge acts were now in demand there. So I taped a few weeks of the Los Angeles radio show ahead and took off for Vegas.

The first time I had appeared in Las Vegas was with Spike Jones in 1947, at Bugsy Siegel's Flamingo. At that time there were only three hotel-casinos on the Strip: the Flamingo, the old Frontier, and the El Rancho Vegas. In those days all the gambling customers came from Northern and Southern California and Colorado, with one plane daily from Chicago. The "restaurant" at the Las Vegas airport at the time consisted of a hot dog machine turning hot dogs on a spit. That's all that some of the visitors after leaving the tables could afford—a last supper for twenty-five cents.

The next hotel-casino to open up on the Strip was the Desert Inn. Then came the Sahara, the Sands, the Tropicana, and then the recent explosion of huge new glambling palaces.

In the early days of entertainment in Las Vegas I met a wonderful gentleman who is still a dear friend—Hank Greenspun, editor of the Las Vegas *Sun*. During the last twenty-five years he's become the No. 1 spokesman in publicizing Las Vegas. He's loved by all the stars of show business, as well as the executives of the Las Vegas gambling community. And I admire him because he's always been in the forefront of the fight for Israel's survival.

But in 1953 Las Vegas was still fighting the *Civil War* as far as ethnic shows were concerned. So instead of taking a "Jewish" show to Las Vegas, I decided to take an absolutely superb jazz band. Mannie Klein was busy in the studios and couldn't go, but I got Ziggy Elman, Maurie Stein, Sammy Weiss. . . .

The idea of my playing Las Vegas with an entertaining jazz group had actually come from my friend "Bookie" Levin, the man who originated the whole idea of cocktail-lounge music in this country. That's where he got his nickname of Bookie—from booking musical groups, not horses.

Bookie Levin was a widely respected agent, but he didn't have the clout necessary to pull the Las Vegas doors open wide enough to admit Mickey Katz—even with my jazz band. The house talent booker at the Frontier, where

Bookie had been presenting me as a possible new act, said I was "too Jewish."

Enter Milton Deutsch, who was formerly Woody Herman's manager and later Rowan & Martin's agent. The owners of the Frontier were Milton Stevens, a young executive from Chicago, and Jake Kosloff, a gentleman gambler from Reading, Pennsylvania. Milton Deutsch went to see them and said, "Let's cut out this bullshit about Mickey Katz being too Jewish. Mickey and that great band of his can please any audience."

So over their own house booker's objections, the owners of the Frontier took a chance and booked me for two weeks with options. We were such a hit that by the end of the first week my contract was renewed for an additional four weeks, and I ended up staying eighteen weeks.

As I said, we were doing a musical act. If someone came in and asked me to perform one of my English-Yiddish parodies, I'd do it, but we were not doing an ethnic show.

That reminds me of a story. At a luxury hotel in Las Vegas the phone rang at four A.M. in the room of a gentleman swinger.

An unhappy little lady's voice on the phone asked, "Is this Sam?"

"Yes," he said, "this is Sam. Who's talking?"

"This is Sadie talking."

"Sadie," he said. "Sadie, Sadie, Sadie. . . . With which Sadie am I having the pleasure?"

"This is the Sadie," she said unhappily, "with who you already had the pleasure."

Still he couldn't remember her. "So give me a hint, give me a for-instance."

"This is the Sadie you met at Miami Beach. Remember, we hullyed together. You always said I was such a good sport."

"Oh-ho!" He remembered. "Sadie, the good sport! What's cooking, *bubele?*"

"What's cooking! I'm pregnant, I'm going to have a baby,

and I'm going to kill myself!"

He said, "By George, Sadie, you *are* a good sport!"

In my show at the Frontier I did a Scottish number I'd written called "McNakatz's Band." I sang it in a strong Scottish burr, with just a word or two of Yiddish for flavoring. As I marched up and down, I sang:

> *Oh, m' name is McNakatz*
> *And I'm the leader of the band.*
> *I play every bar mitzvah*
> *And wedding in the land.*
> *We play for the Poltaver*
> *And the Litvisher Farein;*
> *And shorr it's a Michaye*
> *When a sher they hock arein . . .*

After "McNakatz's Band," Ziggy Elman would stand up and do "Bublichki" and destroy the people, because he was a fabulous player. Then Ziggy would wail "And the Angels Sing" on his trumpet and kill them all over again.

Then Maurie Stein would get up and do a tenor sax solo, "Talk of the Town," of which he'd made a hit record. Sammy Weiss would follow with a tremendous drum solo. And then I'd play "Clarinet Marmalade" and "I Found a New Baby." We did a great show for the simple reason that I had the finest musicians on the West Coast. To close the show, we played a wild *frailach,* and the joint would rock.

While we were at the Frontier, we had one "almost Jewish" incident. One night a huge Texan came up to the bandstand after one of our jazz numbers and said to me, "Hey, boy, how about playing some of that Jew music?"

There was a pregnant silence. Sammy Weiss came up out of his seat at the drums, holding his cymbal, ready to hit him. I held Sammy back and said quietly to the man, "What do you mean—Jew music?"

He said, "Why, them *frailachs.* I haven't heard me a good *frailach* since my bar mitzvah down in Waco."

He was a Texas Hebrew! We all relaxed and played him some Jewish jazz.

We alternated on the bandstand with the incomparable Mary Kaye Trio. We did our show at ten, twelve, two, four, and six (that's six in the morning!). The Mary Kaye Trio came on at eleven, one, three, and five.

Together, we were the hottest lounge attraction in Vegas at that time. When the other hotels—the Flamingo, the El Rancho, the Desert Inn, the Sands—would close their big shows at two A.M., everybody would come over to our place, and we'd be jammed till daylight. In our audience you would see Jack Carter, Judy Garland, Jan Murray, Gordon MacRae, Sammy Davis, Myron Cohen, Sam Levenson. . . .

Humorist Sam Levenson, starring in one of the big Strip hotels, was getting a lot of money. I remember asking him one night how he was getting along at the gaming tables (where many of the stars lost their whole salaries). Sam replied in Yiddish, *"Ich nem mit* [I'm taking mine home]."

Personally, I gambled in Las Vegas only once in my life and then only to teach my son Ronnie a lesson. While I was in Las Vegas with Grace, Ronnie would come in every weekend. He was seventeen and going to school in Los Angeles, but he enjoyed flying over to visit us on the weekends.

Ronnie never gambled, but one night he came into our room and said he'd tried his luck at blackjack and lost $12. He wasn't unhappy about it; he'd tried gambling, found it wanting, and got it out of his system.

But that wasn't good enough for Papa. I got up and said sternly, "Ronnie, we're going to go back down there, and I'm going to win your twelve dollars back for you. *Then* I don't want you to gamble anymore."

So we marched back down to the blackjack table where he'd played, and in trying to get his $12 back, I lost $90. Finally, Ronnie smilingly led *me* away. "Come on, Dad," he said, "let's get out of here. Enough is enough."

There's one other funny bit about Las Vegas, concerning what you might call a fraternal gesture. When an executive of one of the hotel-casinos goes over to visit an executive or owner of one of the other hotel-casinos, it is customary for him to make what is called a laydown, meaning that sometime during the visit he goes past one of the gambling tables and makes a few bets—"invests a little"—as a simple business courtesy.

Well, the house talent booker at the Flamingo was an old friend of mine, Dave Siegel. He came over to see my show one night, and after my performance he remembered that he hadn't made his laydown. Dave was not a big gambler. So he went to the nearest blackjack table, and thinking to get his laydown over with in a hurry, he bet $50. Instead of losing, he won. So he bet $100. And won. Two hundred. And won. Finally, instead of losing a courtesy couple of hundred, he'd won $5000! He was embarrassed. He told his host quite honestly that he'd used up all his time and had to leave, and he left, with the $5000 and a fast goodbye.

While I was at the Frontier, I never worked so hard in my life. We did five shows a night seven nights a week. When I got through at daylight, I was so pooped that all I could do was go next door to the suite that Grace and I had at the Royal Nevada and try to get some sleep. But when I got through work, I was always hungry. So first we'd go past the Chuck Wagon. At least our daylight breakfast-dinner didn't cost much. At the Chuck Wagon a whole gourmet buffet cost a dollar. You could eat a whole prime rib dinner for a buck!

Today in Las Vegas the lounge acts and musicians have it a lot easier. Instead of five shows seven nights a week, they do two shows six nights a week. It should have happened to me.

I first played Las Vegas in 1953; then I went back again in '54 and '55. After the third engagement I bought a new 1956 Cadillac. I mention this for reasons that will become apparent in a moment. After closing at Las Vegas in 1955, I was to open at Harrah's at Lake Tahoe the very next night. So when I got off the stage in Vegas at six in the morning, Grace and I got in our new Cadillac and took off for Tahoe while it was still dark, driving through that gorgeous Nevada scenery by moonlight, with the stars spilling down over us like sparklers at a Fourth of July picnic.

I have many memories of that first engagement at Harrah's at Lake Tahoe. The lake was beautiful—nobody thought of the word "blue" till they saw Lake Tahoe—but the mineral-well drinking water murdered us. Louis Armstrong was playing in the big room, with Myron Cohen. I remember talking to Louis one day and saying, "Louis, are you all right? Are you running to the can the way I am?"

He said, "All the boys in the band are sick. But, Mickey, when it comes to sickness, I just don't accepts it." What a great attitude he had! When it came to sickness, he just didn't "accepts it."

Louis had a philosophy all his own. Alternating in the lounge with us was the now-famous act the Treniers—great musicians and dancers. On opening night one of the young Treniers went into a coffee shop around the corner—and the manager wouldn't serve him because he was black. He came crying and yelling backstage to where I was talking to Louis. He said, "Louis, those bastards in that coffee shop next door won't let me sit down to have anything to eat! They want me to take it out in a bag!"

Louis Armstrong dropped a loving and comforting arm around his shoulders. He said, "Little friend, our time will come, but it is not yet."

During my first and later Lake Tahoe engagements my biggest fan was Bill Harrah's father, who loved my alto sax solos on "Sophisticated Lady," "Josephine," and the other sax classics. He'd come in and sit there, entranced.

Three years ago Grace and I went back to Tahoe to see Joel perform at the new Harrah's Hotel. When I first played Tahoe, Harrah's was just a casino—no hotel at all. Today there's no finer hotel in the world than the new Harrah's.

The rooms are an adventure in luxury. Each room has two bathrooms, with a television set and a phone in each one! Every room has an automatic bar; you push buttons, and out comes scotch, vodka, a little Manischewitz. . . .

Grace and I stayed four days in that magnificent room at Bill Harrah's new hotel. After we checked into the room, the desk called and said, "Mr. Harrah remembers you and particularly how much his father liked your music. You will be his guest during your stay with us." Bill Harrah is loved by all the stars for his thoughtfulness and generosity during their engagements at Harrah's.

My most vivid memory of my first engagement at Lake Tahoe was watching the deer and the antelope play. We did six shows a night at Harrah's, from midnight to six in the morning. I didn't want to live too close to the casino because the nearby motels and other lodging quarters were like barracks at that time. So Grace and I lived up the road about fifteen miles, going toward the North Shore, at a beautiful old landmark called the Glenbrook Country Club. In addition to the golf course, it had a venerable old hotel, one of the most beautiful natural spots I've ever seen.

And did it have deer! The whole area at that time had signs posted everywhere on the roads telling you to be careful of the deer. Not, as it turned out, that you might hurt the deer, but that the deer might hurt you! One night on the way to work a little before midnight, I came around a bend in the road to make the turn into the South Shore, and right there in front of me were about ten big elk. I guess they were elk; they were huge stags with big antlers. They looked as big as elephants. I braked to a stop, and they surrounded the car and looked in at me. I don't think they recognized me.

I couldn't move the car one way or another. And on this lonely road at midnight there were no other cars. I had been warned by the people at the country club not to try to move if deer surrounded the car because with their big antlers they could wreck your car—*and you*. The thing to do was to turn off your lights, DON'T HONK THE HORN, and sit there quietly and wait for them to go away.

So I sat there quietly—and terrified. They'd walk around the car—my splendid new Cadillac—poke at it with their huge horns, even lift up the back end. . . .

After twenty-five of the most agonizing minutes of my life they finally went away.

But how beautiful were the same deer when they weren't too close. Grace and I would often take a little walk at eight or nine o'clock at night before I went to work, and on that Glenbrook golf course there would be a thousand deer. It was as though all the deer in the world were having a convention. That's where they should have been the night the ten horny elk were shopping for a new Cadillac!

10 · I Meet
Some Alter Cockneys
and
Ronnie Calls Collect

THE NEXT YEAR, 1956, I became a Continental Kitten. I went to England and Australia.

But first I had to get a passport. And for me it turned out to be a problem. When the deal was completed for me to go to England, Grace and I were in Buffalo, where I was playing at the twenty-five-hundred-seat Town Casino. We immediately wired the Cleveland city hall to send us our birth certificates. Grace got hers back right away by return mail, but I was told that there was no birth certificate for Mickey Katz, born June 15, 1909. I had, of course, also inquired about my other first names—neither was there a birth certificate for any little boy born on that date named Meyer Katz or Myron Katz. The closest thing was a birth certificate for a Meyer Victor Katz. But that couldn't be mine. Victor was my older brother Al's middle name.

What had happened was that my folks had named my older brother Abraham Victor Katz, and when I'd come along, forgetting that they'd already given Abe (later Al) the middle name of Victor, they'd named me Meyer Victor Katz.

Now during this exchange of correspondence, wires, and phone calls, Grace and I had flown down to New York City, where we were hoping to take the boat for Europe. But the State Department passport office in New York said that it couldn't accept a birth certificate for Mickey Katz made out in the name of Meyer Victor Katz.

So what should I do now? I had to get an older member of the family to say dot's me. My Uncle Izzy came over from Brooklyn, raised his hand over my head, and intoned, "This is Meyer Victor Katz." The passport was finally made out to Mickey Meyer Victor Katz.

Today this is a joke to my grandchildren, who call me on the phone and say, "Hello, Meyer Victor?"

But I finally got the passport in time to make the boat, the old *Île de France*. What a fabulous ship. The food was sensational; the chefs really put their best skillet forward. My nervous little stomach just ate and purred.

But the cabins we'd been assigned were something else. We were going to be accompanied on the trip by our good friends Betty Gallahou and her husband, Murray. When we first looked at our tiny inside cabins, I thought, oh, boy, a midget couldn't get in.

So I used a little musical clout with the purser—promising to entertain at the captain's dinner—and immediately we had two beautiful outside cabins. Incidentally, I entertained at the captain's dinner three times—in first class, cabin class, and tourist—as the captain made his rounds to appear before all his passengers. The French orchestra also followed us around. When I started my "Jewish Mule Train" and handed the whip to the French orchestra leader, he had a fine time cracking the whip and mule calling in French. I, of course, had my clarinet along, and I played jazz, Irish reels, and French and Italian songs. I was a hit in four languages, in three classes.

Betty Gallahou was a funny gal. She enhanced our ocean trip by telling great stories. She told one about a young couple who were going together in Brooklyn. They had been keeping company for fifteen years, with no sign of marriage. One night they would go to the theater, the next night to a social club, the next night to the Sholem Aleichem Society, and the next night to the synagogue. And each night, when he took her home, they would shake hands at the door and say, "Good night, David." "Good night, Sadie."

Well, after fifteen years of this, something had to give. One night, when David took her home and she put out her hand to say good night, he grabbed her hand and put it right on his handle.

She cried out, "To me you would do a doity thing like this! Do you know what my father, the president of the synagogue, would say if he knew what you did to me?"

David pleaded, "Give me a chance to say two words!"

She said, "Shut up. And my mother, the president of the Boro Park Hadassah, what would she say?"

In anguish David said, "Please give me a chance to say *two words!*"

"What is it?"

He screamed, "Let go!"

On the way to London, since we were landing at Le Havre, we sidetracked to Paris. Bobby Weiss, European publicity man for Capitol Records, arranged our Paris stay. The first night, with his date, film star Gloria De Haven, he took us to the craziest restaurant I've ever seen. Each wonderful French roll was shaped like a penis. It was the first time I ever ate a penis. With sweet butter—not bad! Even the ice cream for dessert was cocky-shaped, and the girls suddenly started to scream. The waiter hurried over, and with a great show of Gallic concern, he pulled a live goat out from under the table. On cue the goat had started nibbling at the girls under their dresses! He was a real oversexed old goat.

That reminds me of a crazy joke. A man went to a fine tailor to get measured for a new suit. Before the tailor started measuring him, the man said, "There is something

I have to tell you. I have a problem. I have five penises.
Will the pants fit?"
The tailor said, "Like a glove."

When our plane from Paris landed in England, we had
a royal greeting—from Capitol Records bigwigs and re-
porters and photographers from every newspaper and jazz
publication in London. But when we got to our hotel—the
Washington Hotel on Curzon Street—our rooms had no
baths. I marched down to the manager to complain. I announced, "I'm Mickey Katz."
He gave me a typical British retort. He said, "I don't
know any Mickey Katz, but I've heard of Mickey Mouse. Is
that you, old boy?"
But that night we had rooms with baths.
I had been booked into England by a promoter named
Willy Stephany, plus the William Morris Agency. Willy
Stephany was a delight. He was known as the Mickey Katz
of London. His favorite expression was "That's lovvvvvvvv-
vvvely." He was a little Jewish cockney. Since *alter cocker*
in Yiddish means an over-the-hill, bye-bye boychik, I called
Willy an alter cockney.
Willy had booked me into England to do a tour of single
dates, plus some radio and television shows. My records
were well-known over there; Jack Hilton played them every
day over the BBC. Incidentally, nobody in England had any
fright over anything "Jewish." I was introduced on Britain's
national television as "Mickey Katz, the great Hebrew comedian from Amerrrrica."
After my arrival Willy naturally began introducing me to
important people who were sponsoring my various appearances. Willy would say, "Mickele, this is Cedric Goldberg of
the Cockfoster Synagogue." It so happened that Betty Gallahou was stricken with the "European turistas," meaning the
trots. So when we were introduced to Mr. Cedric Goldberg
of the Cockfosters, she said, "Cockfoster? What I'd like to
do is cock a little slower."

Let me tell you about my musicians for the English dates. Willy, who was himself a fine musician, had listened carefully to my records, then had hired six English musicians who emulated the sound of the band I had had in the States. So for once when I was without my own band, my musicians were great. Good old Willy. "Lovvvvvvvvvely!"

On Sunday nights the regular Palladium vaudeville show was closed. However, there was a television show live every Sunday night from the Palladium stage, called—what else— *Sunday Night at the Palladium.*

The Sunday night I was to make my debut from the Palladium on British telly I was delayed after a previous appearance at a private party. I grabbed a cab and went rushing to the Palladium. After I did my act, the applause was most generous. Excited from all of this, I walked off the stage into the darkened backstage area, right into a piece of scenery, and gave one of my testicles such a bang it was not a question. By the time I got back to my hotel I had one ball and one basketball.

A frantic phone call to Willy Stephany shortly brought a dignified knock on the door. Grace admitted a tall, urbane gentleman in a bowler hat, with a little black bag and a tightly rolled umbrella hooked over his arm. He quickly decided that I must be the patient—since I was the only one lying on the couch in agony. He walked over and said, "I am Dr. Weinberg; I have come to look at your parts."

He lifted up the blanket, looked, and said, "Oh, my." At least he didn't start singing "You've got a lovely bunch of coconuts."

Dr. Weinberg ministered to my case of one-sided elephantiasis with great good cheer and medical talent, and in a day or two he had me on my feet and able to carry on. But his official solicitude wasn't over. Several weeks later, when we were leaving England to fly back to the States, Dr. Weinberg arrived unannounced at the airport to join those seeing us off. Farewells and airplane rides both make me nervous, so while waiting for departure time, I decided to go to the men's room. Dr. Weinberg said that he'd just pop along to the WC with me.

One of my fans suddenly noticed my absence.

"Where's Mickey?" he asked.

Another member of the party replied that I'd gone to the can.

Then came the inquiry "Where's Dr. Weinberg?"

The reply: "He's gone to the can with Mickey."

"What's he doing in the can with Mickey?"

"He's taking a last look at his balls."

The other gentleman quipped, "There'll be 'ell to pay if a bobby catches them."

One of my memorable London shows took place at the Stoke Newington Town Hall. Willy told me that I was going to do a performance there for a group of very Orthodox people, which isn't particularly my bag. My shows tend to be a little informal; sometimes they can even get a bit spicy.

When I arrived at the Town Hall at Stoke Newington, there were some eight hundred senior citizens waiting for the performance by Mickey Katz. They had all paid the equivalent of $2 to see me, which in 1956 was an awful lot of money for a theater ticket in England. All the gentlemen were wearing their *yarmulkes* (skullcaps). The stern looks on their faces said, "Make us laugh, Katz, but nothing offensive." Before I could even finish my first joke, someone called out from the audience, "Would you mind covering your head, old boy?" This wasn't an audience; it was a jury.

I put on a *yarmulke* and finished my act to warm applause, but the evening was uphill all the way. I wouldn't have believed that I could have a problem entertaining a Jewish audience, but Stoke Newington was not only too British, but too Jewish for me.

I found out that my next performance was to be at a bar mitzvah. I protested, "Willy, a British bar mitzvah! What are they going to serve—gefilte fish and chips? I thought I was only going to play theaters."

Patiently he said, "You've never seen a bar mitzvah like this one."

And he was right. The bar mitzvah boy was the son of Mickey Gershelick, the "Biscuit King of England." Biscuits (cookies) are big business in England. My namesake, Mickey Gershelick, was a very successful man.

The Gershelick home was about an hour's train ride out of London, on the southeast coast at a town called Westcliff. We checked into the quaint little Westcliff Hotel; late that afternoon Willy picked us up in a chauffeured Bentley and drove us out to the Gershelick home. It was a fabulous country estate, with tables set up all over a huge lawn.

It was certainly a bar mitzvah such as I'd never seen. First we were greeted by a compere, a uniformed announcer who stood at the entrance wearing a chestful of medals. We gave him our names, and he announced to the hundreds of guests: "MR. AND MRS. MICKEY KATZ—FROM AMERRRRRICA!"

As we went on in, a ten-piece orchestra played a few welcoming bars of "America, the Beautiful." There were seven hundred guests. They looked like a nice friendly crowd, my kind of folks; like family. We had hundreds of introductions to charming people.

Then Mr. and Mrs. Gershelick came over to welcome us. He was a handsome man in his early forties, six feet tall; his wife was beautiful; and their son was a nice-looking, well-adjusted thirteen-year-old boy. No pimples.

After a certain amount of talking and drinking, my bladder sent me an emergency message: Now is the time, Mickele. In this whole twenty-two-room Victorian house there was just one bathroom. Later I asked Mr. Gershelick, "How is it that in this magnificent house you have only one bathroom? In my small apartment in Los Angeles we have two."

He said, "What a waste."

Mr. Gershelick had hired a *minyan,* ten religious men, all wearing *yarmulkes.* They conducted evening prayers for at least forty-five minutes.

Then, with the Sabbath over, we started to eat. The waiters served the finest kosher repast I've ever had in my life, including the most delicious poached salmon I have ever tasted. During the dinner the orchestra played for dancing.

After the feast was over, the compere called everyone to order and ceremoniously presented young Master Gershelick. Mickey Gershelick stood there with his arm around his son, and he delivered a beautiful fatherly talk—to him and to the seven hundred guests who were witnessing this beautiful ceremony of a boy publicly accepting his responsibilities of manhood. (The bar mitzvah boy's impressive reading of the Torah had taken place that morning at services at the synagogue in Westcliff.)

Then Mr. Gershelick introduced some of his distinguished guests. There were probably ten Members of Parliament, each of whom made a short but warm address to the youngster, all in the most delightful Oxford English. Most of these prominent guests were Jewish; some were not; they were just good friends who had come to honor Mickey Gershelick.

Then the evening was turned over to entertainment, and MC Willy Stephany introduced me to a standing ovation. I gave them an hour's performance, after which they gave me another round of cheers.

When we got back to the Savoy Hotel in London, the hotel phone operator said that my son Ronnie had been trying to call me collect from Los Angeles. I told the operator that of course I'd accept the call, and in a few minutes Ronnie was on the line.

He knocked me out with his opening zinger. He said, "Hello, Dad, I want to get married to Maddie Guttleman."

Grace, at my side, was overhearing this and commenting, "He's so young. Can't he wait a little while?"

So I was suddenly listening to Ronnie with one ear, listening to Grace with the other ear, and in between I was thinking of Ronnie as a very small boy. When Ronnie was

five, Joel was nine and already a star at the Cleveland Playhouse—dramatic raves in the papers about him; all Cleveland showering him with praise. Ronnie was just a five-year-
old kid, acting like any other five-year-old.

But I always tried to let Ronnie know that he and Joel
held an equal place in my heart. When I'd come home at
two o'clock in the morning from playing at the Alpine Village, Grace and Joel would be in bed asleep. But as I closed
the front door, I'd say very quietly, "Where's Ronnie?"
Ronnie would come down those stairs like a shot, in his Dr.
Denton pajamas. And Ronnie and I, just the two of us,
would raid the refrigerator together.

Later I thought I'd failed Ronnie. When he was a young
teenager going to school, I was lonesome traveling on the
road, and I'd take Ronnie out of school so that he and Grace
could travel with me. His school would make up several
months of assignments for him, and he'd travel with us and
study in our hotel rooms, except for the times when we'd
hit Miami Beach, where for a few weeks or months he'd
enter high school. Fortunately, he was as bright as a new
penny, and somehow he kept getting wonderful grades.
Even at the age of fourteen, Ronnie had a computer mind.
At night he'd stand out in front of the theater, mentally
counting the crowd as the customers streamed in. Just before curtain time he'd come backstage and say, "Dad, we'll
have eleven hundred people in the house tonight." He
never missed by more than twenty or thirty tickets.

As I was reliving these memories, I was listening to Ronnie on the phone, and Grace at my elbow was saying,
"What's the hurry—they're both so young. They're so
young."

As a matter of fact, we had met Maddie several times and
thought she was something special. She was beautiful,
bright, and from a fine family.

Ronnie was talking away on the phone, but I was thinking of yet another way I had failed him. Ron has always
loved deep-sea fishing. When I'd be playing in Miami

Beach, Ronnie would get himself a job as a member of the crew of a fishing boat, just so he could go deep-sea fishing. But with my ridiculously weak stomach, I've never been able to go deep-sea fishing with my son. At that moment I deeply regretted it.

Incidentally, Ronnie never wanted to be in any of my shows. He was a good-looking boy, with a fine singing voice, but he was never stagestruck.

And now here he was grown up, a senior in college, and telling me that he wanted to get married. With Grace recovering from this surprise phone call, I said, "Ronnie, are you sure that you want to get married? You're only nineteen years old."

He said, "Yes, I love Maddie, and I want to get married."

I said, "But you don't have any means of support, anything at all. How are you going to do this?"

His only answer was, "Daddy and Mother, *please,* I want to get married."

Before Grace could give out with any more advice, I said, "All right, Ronnie, I want you to get married. When we get home, we'll plan the wedding."

"We want to be married in December."

I replied, "Wonderful." He talked to his mother lovingly for a minute; then we hung up, and Grace and I had a little heart-to-heart misunderstanding.

Grace said, "Ronnie get married! How can you approve of this? He hasn't got any money! He's only nineteen!"

I retorted, "Grace, how old were we when we got married? You were barely eighteen, and I was barely twenty. How much money did we have? We had *bobkes* [nothing]. Except each other."

I finished playing my dates in England—and I must tell you a funny incident. The big kosher restaurant in London's East End—its oldest Jewish neighborhood—was called Bloom's. One noon I took a half dozen people who were sponsors of my concerts over there for lunch because everybody had said, "This is the place, Mickey, where you'll get the finest borscht, the finest flanken and chicken soup in all of England."

When we walked in, it was like walking into Katz's (no relation) Delicatessen on Houston Street on New York's Lower East Side. During World War II, when everybody was sending deli packages to their sons overseas, Katz's deli gave a lot of people a needed laugh with a big sign across the front of their place: BUY A SALAMI FOR YOUR BOY IN THE ARMY.

Anyway, Bloom's waiters in London were just like New York waiters—flatfooted, independent, the aprons practically up to their chins. When we finished our kosher klambake, I asked for the check. It was for two pounds, at that time around $8—for eight people! When I paid it, I asked the waiter to bring me a receipted bill. He said, "What do you want that for?" When I said that I needed it for a tax write-off at home, he went back to the cashier and came back with a receipted bill for a hundred and seventy pounds—around $700!

"Here, Mickele," he said, "save a lot of taxes."

Can you imagine the IRS holding still for a $700 write-off for eight people having a deli lunch!

Then we came home for the summer. In September Grace and I and Mannie Klein and his wife, Dopey, left for Australia. (Nobody knows why Mannie Klein's wife is nicknamed Dopey. She's one of the biggest contractors of musicians in Hollywood.)

The Australian promoters wanted me over there in 1956, because that was the year of the Olympics. I never saw the Olympics, but I certainly enjoyed Australia. Except getting there. In 1956 there were no jets, and travel from Los Angeles to Australia in a prop plane was a murderous trip.

It took twenty-seven hours. We stopped at every island except Coney.

We were booked for four weeks, at good salaries, plus transportation and hotels for all four of us. We landed at Sydney, ready for work, but the first week we didn't do anything! We stayed at a small hotel called the Chelsea, in King's Cross, which in 1956 was Sydney's theatrical and restaurant district. We'd been brought over by a combine of three Australian Jewish boys and one gentile associate— Sammy Weiss, Wolfie Pizan, Rickey Ahlberger, and Ron Bennett—and they didn't seem to have things too well organized. I think this was their first promotion, and it looked as if it might be their last. There was a wonderful, adventurous spirit in Australia; our hosts seemed to be making up the tour as they went along. So far they seemingly hadn't thought of where to start.

So while the promoters were getting ready to promote, the Katzes and the Kleins enjoyed Sydney. It was a city a great deal like San Francisco, even to "the bridge" and the good eating. At our little Chelsea Hotel we had our own waiter, who brought us great international goodies. And King's Cross had many other wonderful restaurants—Hungarian, Polish, Italian, Russian, whatever you had in mind.

And between restaurants we sampled the delis. The Australian delis were so cosmopolitan that you'd see in one window a Jewish salami, a Polish salami, an Italian salami, and a Hungarian ham. Whatever you wanted, they had it. And we got it.

After a week of slaving away like this, we drew our first week's wages. We'd had nice write-ups in the papers every day, but so far we hadn't played anywhere!

Then our hosts said, "We're going to take you to Melbourne tomorrow and show you where you're going to play there." So we flew down to Melbourne, a very "British" city. Our Melbourne host was Wolfie Pizan, who today is Australia's most prominent restaurateur. After a day or two of our enjoying Melbourne, Wolfie said he was going to take us to a club that was something special, where there were quite a few Jewish people.

He took us to a nightclub called the Moulin Rouge, and we took our instruments along. It was a strange name for the place; the audience was three hundred newly arrived Polish refugees, all speaking Yiddish. After an hour of watching them dance waltzes, I said, "Mannie, why don't we take out our horns and play these people some *frailachs?*"

You must remember that these refugees from Europe hadn't heard any Jewish music since 1939, when Poland was invaded. This was 1956, seventeen years later.

The bandleader and his four musicians were Italian. I asked him to play a *frailach* rhythm background in B flat. He said, *"No parle inglese,"* which in American means "No spika de English." I looked at Mannie. What do we do now?

Mannie thought a minute and then said, "Let's try the do-re-mi system on him."

I said, "Maestro, *re bi mol* [B flat in Italian]."

Suddenly he understood, and said, *"Che tempo* [What tempo]?" We sang it for him: bomp de bomp de bomp— bomp de bomp de bomp. And they started playing the rhythm—on accordion, bass, and saxophone. Then Mannie and I joined in on clarinet and trumpet, in a medley of exciting horas and *frailachs*.

The audience looked at each other in disbelief. It was Jewish music! There were squeals of delight as the women kicked off their shoes and ran out on the dance floor, the men joined them, and they began to dance. They didn't stop till we had to stop for breath, and then they were all over us—hugging us, kissing us, the tears rolling down. It was an emotional evening I'll never forget.

Then we flew back to Sydney, where we were to open at the Coliseum for two shows—our first actual work of the whole tour.

At our hotel in Sydney there was a wire waiting for Mannie; his brother was in serious condition in Los Angeles after a heart attack. Mannie felt that he should go back. After our hosts had paid the fare to Australia for him and his wife and we hadn't played a single show yet!

But our Australian hosts said, "If he has to go back, he has to go back."

I did my best to emulate their carefree attitude. But as

much as I sympathized with Mannie, I was left without a conductor and trumpet soloist familiar with my act. With a tour still ahead of me.

Since there was nothing else I could do, I hired a local conductor and did the two shows at the Sydney Coliseum, and business was amazingly good. I say amazingly because at that time there were only twenty-five thousand Jews in all Sydney. But we packed in about twelve hundred a show for the two shows, our hosts made a few thousand dollars, and everybody was happier.

There's an ancient synagogue in Sydney that's more than a hundred years old. It's really something to see. Before starting on my shows, I thought that I should go over there, meet some of the people, and let them see Mickey Katz. Promoter Ron Bennett, an Irish-Catholic, said, "That's a good idea." Turning to Wolfie Pizan, he said, "Wolfie, why don't you take Mickey over to the synagogue?"

Wolfie replied, "I don't want to go to any synagogue."

To which Ron Bennett exploded, "Well, who the hell do you think is going to take him to the bloody synagogue— *me?*"

I ended up going by myself. When the worshipers recognized me from my picture in the papers, I was given a royal welcome. At least fifty people wanted to take me to their homes for a little *kiddush* (a glass of wine) and a *Shabbes* lunch.

I played three more shows in Sydney to packed houses. Then I went to Melbourne. My hosts figured I would do three or four shows there, but they put me into a huge amphitheater called the Arena, and I played to four thousand people in one night! Which was all the business there was for us in Melbourne.

Now they didn't know what to do with me. I still had two weeks to go on my contract. With all our round-trip fares over there, I knew the promoters must be out at least $5000. But the Jewish communities in Adelaide and Brisbane were too small for me to play there, and the transportation clear across Australia to Perth was prohibitive.

So for the next ten days Grace and I just had a wonderful time as visitors in Melbourne and Sydney. When it came time to settle up and leave for home, Wolfie Pizan and Sammy Weiss said, "What do we do about Mannie's and Dopey's air transportation [which came to around $1500]?"

I said, "Boys, what do you want me to do? It was an act of God."

Wolfie, Sammy, Rickey, and Ron looked at each other; then one of them said, "What the hell? We enjoyed having you over here; the shows went well; the deal didn't cost us enough to cry about." And they paid me in full.

The last night before Grace and I left Sydney I held a party for them at the Chelsea, and there were a lot of mutual and very sincere toasts and good wishes.

I must tell you about two other events that made the trip memorable. I've told you how comparatively few Jewish people there are in all Australia. But every year they have a Flag Day for the Jewish National Fund. I was in Melbourne on Flag Day. Little Jewish kids were standing out on the street corners with little flag-decorated donation cans. And in a country that's 95 percent non-Jewish, *all* the Australians were putting in some money! To help Israel. The Australians love Israel because the Israelis too are a pioneering people.

Then there was one unforgettable night in Melbourne. After my show Wolfie Pizan said that a friend of his wanted to take Grace and me out to his home. We got into this man's car and drove out about twenty miles to his large country estate. The house was dark. When we got out of the car, he said, "There's no one home, but just come along. I'll turn on the lights."

We walked up to the house, he opened the door, and in the big darkened living room were at least fifty children, each holding a freshly lit candle and all singing "Hatikvah," the national anthem of Israel.

None of us could speak. What can I tell you? Grace and I were overcome.

We flew home from Sydney. And in December we helped Ron and Maddie with their wedding. It was a beautiful wedding. We expected three hundred at the reception, five hundred came, and in the midst of the proceedings Betty Gallahou, who had flown out from New York, noticed that the bartenders were pouring everybody doubles. She said to the head bartender, "Look, you're going to break Mickey Katz. From now on serve *only singles!*"

Which worked fine till Betty went to the bar and ordered a double for herself. The bartender remonstrated, "But you told me to give everybody singles."

Betty said, "Not me, dummy—*them.*"

11 · Nuptials
for Yossel (Joel)
and
Katz in the Katzkills

RON'S MARRIAGE left us with one more wedding to go. But not for long. In the spring of 1958 Joel delighted us by calling from New York to say that he was getting married in June. What a thrill it was to think of Joel also being happily married and starting a family. For us Katzes, it would be another *simcha* (joyous occasion).

Joel's betrothed was a beautiful and talented young actress named Jo Wilder. Joel had met her at a party on the Coast, and just like Papa and brother Ron, once Joel met his future wife there was no question about it. Joel brought her to see us at our apartment, and Grace and I also loved her right from the start. With her name, Jo Wilder, Grace and I didn't know whether she was Jewish or not. At first we didn't think she was; then we found that her grandfather was a rabbi in Brooklyn!

Sitting beside Grace on the plane flying east to the wedding, I was thinking about Joel's boyhood.

Let me tell you one of my memories of Joel as a youngster. After an earlier move to the Coast in 1943 that didn't last long, I moved the family back to Los Angeles in 1946, after I joined Spike Jones. Joel was fourteen. That winter he came down with a debilitating and mysterious virus. Despite our home remedies, he got rapidly worse. He would get into uncontrollable paroxysms of coughing and literally turn blue.

We called a doctor we'd known from Cleveland. He came over, examined Joel, and told us, "Now don't worry. You think that every coughing spell is going to be his last breath, but it isn't. He'll get over this."

The doctor made several more visits, but instead of getting over it, Joel got steadily worse. With the doctor telling us that everything was going to be fine, for six agonizing days Grace and I watched our son simply waste away.

Finally, in desperation we called Grace's cousin Charlie Silver, who had lived in Los Angeles for twenty years. I said, "Charlie, we have to have another doctor for this boy." Charlie called his family physician, who was a doctor of the old school. He came over at once, took one look at Joel, and said, "I would like to strongly propose a drastic emergency measure. I think he should have an immediate blood transfusion from his mother."

He wanted to give Joel a blood transfusion from Grace—and right there in the house! I said, "Shouldn't this be done in a hospital?"

He said, "There's no time. It should be done right now."

So, helpless and not knowing what else to do, we said to go ahead. And there in the house this amazing doctor gave Joel a transfusion of Grace's blood. He didn't type their blood—how could a mother's blood hurt her son? Later other doctors told me that this highly unorthodox procedure could have been fatal to Joel.

Thank God it wasn't. Within hours he was much better! He coughed very little after that; in a few days he went back to school.

And within a year Joel was starring onstage with me in the *Borscht Capades,* and three years later he was working in America's biggest cabarets and nightclubs.

I recently had lunch with black singing star Billy Daniels at the Friars Club, and Billy told me a funny story about the early period of Joel's career. Joel came up to the Catskills looking for work. Billy Daniels, who was starring at Grossinger's, introduced him from the stage as "My friend Mickey Katz's son, Joel Grey." Billy had just finished performing his big number, "Old Black Magic," to his usual thunderous applause.

When he invited Joel to do a number, Joel said, "How about my doing my own version of 'Old Black Magic'?" Somewhat surprised, Billy said to go ahead. Joel had never done the number before, but he proceeded to do "Old Black Magic" exactly as Billy had done it, with all of Billy's famous gyrations, plus some ad-lib Jewish shticks. The audience was destroyed.

The next morning Billy and Joel were walking around the grounds, and a very elderly, nearsighted gentleman came up to them. Shaking hands warmly with Billy Daniels, he said, "Mr. Katz, I think your son is wonderful."

Joel went on to be wonderful at the Copa and a lot of other famous places. With all this fantastic early success, it was inevitable that he would have to pause sometime to catch up with himself. As fate would have it, this pause in his career came just about the time he fell in love with Jo and decided to get married. When Joel married Jo, he was playing casual club dates. But that didn't matter to either one of them. They loved each other, they both knew that great success was out there in the world somewhere, and they determined to capture it together. After their marriage they had a rough time for a while; they lived in a little walk-up apartment in Greenwich Village, and money they didn't have. In fact, they were a little short of cash.

But Joel kept working toward his real aspiration—the Broadway stage—and soon he was playing Hal March's kid brother in *Come Blow Your Horn*. The show ran for five hundred performances on Broadway, and Joel was on his way again. There followed his starring role in the national company of *Stop the World, I Want to Get Off.*

Instead of getting off, Joel got on. Because next came the role of the Master of Ceremonies in Hal Prince's Broadway production of *Cabaret,* for which Joel won the Tony Award.

Following that, Joel created the role of George M. Cohan in the musical "George M," at the Palace Theater on Broadway.

And then came the real blockbuster, the movie of *Cabaret,* which won Oscars for both Joel and Liza Minnelli.

But at the time of his marriage Joel hadn't yet made it this big. Joel and Jo had a small, intimate wedding in New York City in the apartment of close friends. The guests included only the parents, a few of the young couple's close friends—and, not to be forgotten, Jo's grandmother and grandfather, the rabbi.

Grandpa did *not* like what was going on. Before the service Joel told me that they were going to have a Conservative marriage ceremony, and I thought, oh, boy, Grandpa, the Orthodox rabbi, is going to like this just fine!

In an Orthodox marriage ceremony the groom's parents escort him down the aisle to the *chuppa* (the ceremonial canopy over the marriage altar), and the bride's parents escort her down the aisle to the altar.

This was not that kind of service. The kids wanted to be married by a young Conservative rabbi, with the parents standing off to one side. We were in, but we were also out.

When the venerable *zayde* (grandfather) found out what was going to happen, he said emphatically, "The father and mother have got to lead the bride and the groom, separately, down the aisle to the *chuppa*. Otherwise, it's a disgrace!"

I had to become Meyer the Peacemaker. I talked to the grandfather earnestly in Yiddish. I told him in Yiddish, "Look, Grandpa, the children are getting married by a rabbi. They're doing it the way they want it. Let's enjoy with them!"

At one point in the service Joel had to repeat some of the

young rabbi's words in Hebrew about the significance of the wedding ring. As Joel spoke the words in perfect Hebrew, out of left field we heard the old rabbi grandfather call out, "Goot, goot!" He was happy. Then the wedding party went on to dinner at an Italian restaurant called Danny's Hideaway. For Mr. and Mrs. Joel Grey's Jewish wedding dinner, instead of Manischewitz, roast chicken, and flanken, we had Italian wine, lasagna, and chicken Katziatora.

Then the bride and groom took off for their honeymoon, and I took off to play the Catskills—for the first time in my life.

As far as I know, I was the only American Jewish entertainer who had never played the Catskills. But that's the way the matzo ball bounces. I grew up not in New York, but in Cleveland, moved to California, made my reputation, and from then on I never went back east except with my own revues. For me to play any solo dates in the Catskills, the transportation costs for Grace and me, plus the hiring of a great trumpet player to work in my act, made the whole thing impractical.

But when I was making plans to go east for Joel's wedding, I asked my agent, Milton Deutsch, to book some dates in the Catskills. Milton called Charley Rapp, who at that time was "the big Catskills booker," and Charley made a deal at $1500 a week, plus hotels, for nine shows a week for four weeks, with options to Labor Day. I thought it would be a nice vacation for a few weeks following Joel's wedding, so I said okay.

A happy coincidence was that for Grace and me it would be in a way a second honeymoon in the Catskills.

Remember the disastrous days after our marriage when Uncle Louie and Aunt Sadie rescued us from Coney Island? Well, while we were living with them at North Arlington, New Jersey, Uncle Louie loaded Grace and me and Aunt Sadie and their two daughters into his big phaeton car and drove us to the Catskills for a three-day vacation—in Parksville, at a place called Cohen's Farm.

Which reminds me of a joke. A lady guest at one of the Catskills hotels went down to the desk one day to complain. In great anger she told the manager, "The food here is poison—plain, plain poison. And such small portions!"

At Mr. Cohen's wonderful "farm" in 1930, we had large portions of great Jewish delicacies. This simple boardinghouse in the Kosher Highlands was everything that made the Catskills famous.

As I am in no way a historian, let me give you what to my knowledge is the world's shortest history of the Catskills. The Jewish people who first went up to the Catskills, around 1900, went there not for vacations, but for their health. From years of living in the airless New York ghettos and working in the airless New York sweatshops, countless people eventually came down with what they called consumption—tuberculosis.

So various charitable organizations sent them up to the Catskills. The wonderful fresh dry air made them well, and many of them bought little farms and started taking in boarders. With the passing of the years, the boardinghouses became hotels, and the hotels became palaces—such as today's Grossinger's and the Concord, vast complexes with a thousand rooms, fine food and entertainment, even their own golf courses.

Here's one of legendary comedian Mickele Rosenberg's stories about the Catskills.

A man who was an enthusiastic golfer drove up to the Catskills one day, hoping to spend his vacation at a hotel having golf privileges. He first stopped at a beautiful big hotel, which we will call Goldfinger's in the Pines. He got out of his car and went in to the desk and inquired, "Do you have a golf course?"

The desk clerk said, "Yes, we have a beautiful golf course."

Pleased, the man said, "And how much are the rooms here?"

The clerk said, "Sixty-five dollars a day."

Outraged, the man said, "At that price, you shouldn't depend on me!" And he walked out, got back in his car, and drove away.

A few minutes later, on down the road, he came upon a smaller hotel with a big sign out in front saying: ROOMS $5.00 A DAY. GOLF PRIVILEGES."

He immediately checked in.

And for the next week he had a fabulous time, thoroughly enjoying the hotel and the golf course. Till at the end of the week he went to the cashier's desk to pay his bill.

His bill was $743.

He said, "What the hell is this all about it! Are you crazy! Your sign says your rooms are only five dollars a day!"

The cashier said, "That's right. Five dollars a day for seven days—it's right there on your bill—room thirty-five dollars. But let me ask, did you play any golf?"

"Of course I played golf. That's why I'm here."

"By any chance did you use any of our balls?"

"Yes, I wanted to go first class. I bought a half dozen new balls."

The cashier said, "Well, there's our little misunderstanding. Our golf balls cost one hundred seventeen dollars apiece."

The man almost had apoplexy. "For this kind of money I could have stayed at Goldfinger's in the Pines! I'll bet they don't charge you one hundred seventeen dollars for balls."

The clerk said, "No, at Goldfinger's they get you by the *rooms.*"

Which certainly didn't apply to wonderful Cohen's Farm. Remember, this was 1930, but Cohen's provided rooms for the *six* of us for a total of $10 a day, including meals! And such meals! Mr. Cohen was a jovial middle-aged man who always wore golf knickers. At breakfast he would happily make the rounds of the tables, making sure that everybody had enough to eat. Enough? First the waiters brought out beautiful kippers. If you didn't like kippers, they had herring in cream sauce, blintzes with bowls of sour cream, *latkes* (potato pancakes), tremendous platters of lox and eggs, hot bagels and sweet rolls. . . . And Mr. Cohen would pause at each table with a big milk can, with a big ladle, and he'd say, "Come on, kids, have another glass of milk."

A small boy at the table might complain, "If I eat any more, I'll bust."

But his mother would smile understandingly at Mr. Cohen and say, "Give him another glass milk."

No wonder that people of even very modest means would save all year to have that exhilarating vacation in the Catskills.

But Cohen's Farm was 1930. Here I was, twenty-eight years later, a known recording artist, on my way back to the Catskills to entertain new audiences.

I should have stood in bed. I'd had visions of playing only the top spots like Grossinger's, the Concord . . . but unknown to me, the Charley Rapp office, anxious to take in as much money as possible while paying me only my weekly salary, had been booking me not only into the good spots but into every *kochalayn* and boardinghouse from New Jersey to Albany. I didn't realize what I was in for till I rented a car and Grace and I drove up to the Catskills the day before our first date. Our hotel was to be in a village called Woodridge; we were to enjoy gracious mountain living there, while I played a circle of happy engagements in the area.

About noon we arrived at Woodridge. There was a beautiful big motel up on a hill, and I naturally assumed that this was to be our home away from home. I parked the car out in front and went in to get a bellboy.

When the desk clerk found out who I was, he shook hands warmly—and pointed off down the hill to a crummy, moth-eaten old boardinghouse that looked more like an outhouse. *That* was where Charley Rapp housed his Catskills acts, including me.

Grace, in a spirit of adventure, said, "Well, let's take a look."

We drove down the hill—I do mean *down* the hill—and the place where we were supposed to stay was full of starving actors. There's nothing wrong with hungry actors, but it's a shock when you're no longer hungry. Many were still asleep after playing somewhere late the night before. One man came by in a towel on his way to the community shower for twenty people. Everything was not coming up roses. Instead of roses, there was a delicate aroma of stale laundry.

I looked at Grace, she looked at me—and we made our escape. We drove back up the hill and checked in at the nice motel—twenty bucks a day. My twenty bucks. The following day we drove on over and checked into Grossinger's at sixty bucks a day for room and food, and that's where we stayed for the next two weeks, while I started playing my tour of "the Catskills," which in my case turned out to be anything north of Atlantic City. In the morning I'd get a call from the Charley Rapp office, telling me the location of that night's date. If I got an *early* call, I knew I was going quite a ways. One night I was booked at a Jewish country club at Tarrytown, which was one hundred twenty miles away.

After two weeks of it I called up Charley Rapp and said, "After this week, do me a favor and include me out. Some of these jumps should be made by helicopter. This is not for me. Let my people go."

Charley said, "Mickey, before you leave, there's one place I wish you'd play. It's a small hotel near Monticello called Esther Manor. There's an old lady there who's been driving the MC crazy, demanding to know when you're going to appear. So go already."

Esther Manor was the sort of small hotel that Carl Reiner

once told me about. When Carl was a young aspiring actor, seventeen years old, he and some other young performers were booked into a small hotel in the Catskills. They had a tab show—a miniature musical comedy. They were a talented and very jazzy bunch of kids. The audience, however, was nearly all elderly people who would much rather have heard Molly Picon or one of the other traditional Yiddish theater artists.

Carl and his fast-moving musical-comedy group came out like Gangbusters and gave it their best. But the people in the audience looked at each other in mock disbelief. When the performance was over, there was a minimum of polite applause, and Carl knew that he and the others had laid a bomb.

As he walked out into the lobby after the performance—crushed—an elderly gentleman stopped him and said, "Kid, you're good, but not marvelous."

Carl asked, "What do you mean?"

The old gentleman continued: "*Jumbo* at the Hippodrome, with the elephant—dot's marvelous. Caruso—dot's marvelous. Molly Picon—dot's marvelous. But, kid, you're just plain good, not marvelous."

On the night when I finally appeared at Esther Manor, the MC in the bell-bottom white flannels announced me with a great flourish: "And now, ladies and gentlemen, you've been waiting for him for a long time—Mickey Katz!" At which the little old lady who had waited so long for my nonappearance stood up when I entered and said, "So the big shot showed up already. Big deal."

And thus ended the saga of Katz in the Katzkills, playing dates from Fallsburgh to Philadelphia and Liberty to Newark. With fond memories of the Actors' Heaven at Woodridge, better known as Stalag 17.

One final story about the Catskills:

One day at the height of the season there appeared on a vacant lot a big circus tent with a huge sign announcing:

COMING THIS SATURDAY FOR A LIMITED ENGAGEMENT—THE
FAMOUS SAM LEFKOWITZ—THE GREATEST HIGH DIVER IN THE
WORLD—AGE 87!

Well, word of this great coming attraction went around
the Catskills like wildfire, and Saturday about ten thousand
people bought tickets and hurried into the big tent. In the
middle of the tent was a small washtub, with an endlessly
long ladder reaching into the top of the tent.

Precisely at two o'clock there was a thunderous drumroll,
and a spotlight picked up Sam Lefkowitz, the famous high
diver, standing beside the ladder in tights. He was a
wizened, bowlegged little gentleman who looked fully
eighty-seven, but he bowed to the crowd and then began
climbing the long ladder, up and up and up, stopping on
almost every rung to rest. But on he went, up and up.
Finally, he reached the little platform at the very top of
the endless ladder, and before making his perilous dive, he
paused to make a little speech.

He said, "Ladies and gentlemen, you have each paid five
dollars to see me, a man of eighty-seven years, dive off this
platform into that little tub of borscht.

"But before I dive off this platform, let me tell you the
truth. If I make this jump, do you know what is going to
happen? I will break every bone in my body, I will be finished, I will be dead like a dog. Do you want that to happen?"

There were cries of "No . . . no . . . no!"

He said, "Thank you very much. Next show, four
o'clock."

12 · What Am I Doing in Africa!

IN THE FALL of 1960, to my surprise, I got a letter from a man named Percy Tucker, in Johannesburg, South Africa. He wrote that he was interested in bringing me over for a national tour. He said that he would shortly be in America, and he would contact me. I wrote back and said that I would be happy to meet him, though in my own mind I thought who the hell wants to go to Africa.

About a month later my phone rang, and it was Mr. Tucker. In a highly clipped British accent, he said that he had just arrived in New York City and would very much like to come to Los Angeles and discuss a "booking." I said fine, and a few days later he was in Los Angeles.

At that time things were going well with the Katzes; we were living in a penthouse in Westwood. We invited Mr. Tucker over. Grace cooked a lovely dinner, and after dinner Percy said, "You know, your records are quite big among the Jewish people of South Africa, and I'd like to bring you over there for some personal appearances."

I said, "Let me ask you something. How many Jewish people are there in South Africa?"

"A hundred and fifteen thousand."

I said, "If I play a city in the United States with a hundred and fifteen thousand Jewish population, I play one performance."

"You don't know our situation in South Africa. We will play you in Cape Town, Johannesburg, Durban, Port Elizabeth, East London, Pretoria, my hometown of Benoni . . ."

I told him that outside of Cape Town and Johannesburg, I'd never heard of any of those places.

He went on patiently: "In Cape Town we will play a minimum of five performances, six in Johannesburg, and we'll play the other cities for one night. You'll be with us for four weeks."

"How many people do you expect to draw to these concerts?"

"Oh, if we play fifteen dates, we should draw at least twenty-five thousand people."

I said, "Percy, either you're meshuga, or you're the Barnum of Benoni."

He brought things to a head by asking, "How much do you want for your package, and who will be in the cast?"

Well, since the whole thing sounded like a pipe dream, I thought I might as well dream up a first-class deal. I said, "First, I want to engage comedian and vocalist Marty Drake; I want Mannie Klein to conduct the orchestra and to play trumpet solos. My wife, Grace, has to come along, and Mannie won't make the trip without his wife."

He was beginning to look a little concerned. "That many people on the trip might make things a bit high. South Africa isn't a stone's throw, you know. The plane fare for that many people would run six thousand dollars."

"First class?"

"No, first class would run eleven thousand."

"For a fifteen-thousand-mile trip, that's the way I want to go."

He said, "Well, let me consider that. Now what would the package itself cost?"

"I want $2500 a week, plus all expenses for myself and Grace, including a suite at all hotels, plus $750 a week for Marty Drake and $500 a week for Mannie, plus their living expenses and first-class transportation for everyone." I was giving Percy a rough time because I had no desire whatever to go to Africa.

But he wasn't exactly crushed. He said, "I'll let you know."

He got back to South Africa, and within a week I got a letter from a Mr. David Bloomberg in Cape Town, who at the time was Percy's associate in the booking of shows for South Africa. Mr. Bloomberg wrote, "Your deal is accepted. Your tour starts on January 4."

Well, that put it squarely up to me. After conferring with Marty and Mannie, I wired an apprehensive confirmation. And we all left for Africa.

First-class service on the Pan Am jet out of New York for Paris was not to be believed. We were served bottles of the best champagne—Moët & Chandon and Piper-Heidsieck. Then we were served oysters Rockefeller, chateaubriand, artichoke hearts with hollandaise sauce, petit fours, French ice cream with strawberries. . . .

We spent most of our two days in Paris recovering from out gorgeous gluttony. It didn't bother Mannie Klein; with Mannie it's always the season to be jolly. Even on the night we got in he went from club to club with his trumpet. The next day you couldn't get into our hotel, for the French musicians trying to see Mannie. Jazz musicians, symphony musicians, young musicians, old musicians, all came to worship at the Klein shrine.

We left Paris at ten the second night, flying out on the French airline UTA, for South Africa. This was January 1961, during the war in the Belgian Congo. Our first stop, after flying for ten hours, was at Brazzaville, in the French Congo. Only four of our first-class passengers were preparing to get off—two uniformed French officers and two black African diplomats.

Just before we landed, the pilot announced over the plane's loudspeakers, "All passengers continuing on south, don't leave the airport!" The airport was surrounded by a barbed-wire fence and ringed by French Congolese troops.

We went to the little airport restaurant, where we were told we were to have breakfast. I wondered what it would be like.

The French waitress was one of the most beautiful girls I have ever seen. She and her father and mother ran the restaurant. They proceeded to serve us exotic fruits, followed by eggs and crepes suzette—there in the middle of Africa.

As we came out of the restaurant, we noticed that outside the barbed-wire fence, staring in at us, was a group of Bokongo natives—all seven feet tall and all no doubt due to some dietary deficiency completely toothless. They'd come over to the airport, curious to see who was arriving.

Marty Drake, who was half loaded, walked up to the inside of the fence and started a conversation in his version of slang Congo lingo. He addressed one of the big Bokongos, "Kahaboolah?" The guy turned to his cronies and repeated, "Alla kahaboolah?" The others said, "Hawa alla kabugu-bugu." This went on for ten minutes, between the natives and Marty, all of them seeming to enjoy it. I finally went and retrieved Marty, and on the way back to the plane I asked him what he had said to the Bokongos. He said, "I was telling them how disappointed I was; Mom and Dad always meet me in Brazzaville."

Then we got back on the plane and took off for Salisbury, Rhodesia. Rhodesia is a gorgeous scenic country; the famous Victoria Falls are there. As we approached Salisbury, the jungle below us began to disappear and we began to see European-style homes and buildings.

After a thirty-minute service stop at Salisbury we took off for South Africa. By now we were beginning to get tired. We'd been in the air—in a DC-8 jet—for twelve hours. South Africa was indeed not a "stone's throw."

We were to land next at Johannesburg and have a five-hour layover there before flying the five hundred miles on south to Cape Town.

We landed at Johannesburg at one-thirty in the afternoon. Percy Tucker met us at the plane and whisked us off to a beautiful house for lunch and a rest. It was like being at an outstanding home in Southern California, Florida, or Long Island. Such food and service as you can't imagine.

After lunch the members of the press arrived to interview us—a reporter from the Johannesburg *Star,* the editor of the Anglo-Jewish paper for South Africa, and the reviewers from the South African jazz trade papers. In the midst of this meeting with the press I went to sleep.

When I woke up, there was only one newsman left. He said, "The other chaps left to write up your little nap." And one of them did! He wrote: "In the midst of our interview, Mr. Katz started to snore. And though he's a noted musician, I must say he was off-key."

Incidentally, since South Africa is well below the equator, its seasons are the reverse of ours. Summer starts in the winter, and winter starts in the summer. Also, the whites live in the center of the cities, and the blacks live in the suburbs.

That night at eight o'clock we left Johannesburg for Cape Town. To me it seemed like three o'clock in the morning. To Mannie and Marty, it was like noon. They felt no pain. They finished their boozing and started snoozing.

As we were descending over the Cape Town airport, I thought Winston Churchill must be expected! It was ten o'clock at night, but there were searchlights and spotlights all over the place. When we got off the plane, we were given a musical ovation by the most amazing uniformed band you've ever seen—black children playing on washtubs and homemade woodwind instruments and singing a native folk song which went like this: "*Dar kum* [Here comes] Mickey Katz . . . Marty Drake . . . Mannie Klein. . . ." I found out later that the title of this song is "Ala-boma." Funny, I never heard it in Montgomery.

There were even beautiful uniformed little girls who

showered us with flowers. All of it had been arranged by
David Bloomberg. I thought I was in a Disney movie called
South African Fantasia.

The first two days in Cape Town we didn't work at all.
David Bloomberg had reserved us rooms at a fabulous
seventy-six-year-old hotel overlooking the coast, called the
Clifton. I had my own valet there, a black man whose name,
so help me, was Israel. Believe me, he didn't look it. But
what a lovely man! Any time he brought anything to our
room, alongside the plate there would always be a fresh
flower.

Our first concert in Cape Town was in the auditorium of
City Hall. There was a capacity crowd of a thousand people
in the audience, all in formal dress. At the end of the performance they gave us a standing ovation. This country is
not to be believed.

When the show was over, we were driven to the home of
David Bloomberg's parents. David's father was Abe Bloomberg, the former mayor of Cape Town, a Member of Parliament, and an intimate friend of the late Winston Churchill.
(David himself has since served as the mayor of Cape Town.)

In all my life I've never seen such a house—a magnificent
plantation straight out of *Gone with the Wind.* There were
one hundred people present to welcome us—local digni-
taries and community leaders. The Bloombergs served a
scrumptious buffet dinner. There was shrimp, lobster,
chicken, turkey, filet mignon, roast beef, along with all sorts
of tropical fruit and fine wines, many of them from Abe
Bloomberg's own vineyards.

We had a special bonus from David Bloomberg's govern-
mental clout. Before leaving the States, I'd written David
that in addition to my clarinet and Mannie's legendary
trumpet, we would need five other musicians. He drafted
five great musicians for us out of the Royal South African
Navy Band!

Our second concert in Cape Town was at Weizmann
Hall, named in honor of Chaim Weizmann, the first presi-

dent of Israel. Our musical numbers were such a hit that we decided that we should add a little jazz music. So at the finish of our next concert I raised the clarinet and kicked off a chorus of "Honeysuckle Rose." Mannie and the rest of the band joined in, and the joint went up in flames! You've never heard such applause. From then on we included some straight Dixieland jazz in all the concerts, and everybody loved it, particularly the many non-Jewish people we were attracting in our audiences.

David Bloomberg was not only a thoughtful employer, but a fabulous host. He planned our days and nights as though we were guests in his home.

The South African Jewish community has its roots in many countries—Great Britain, Russia, Germany. There are also Jews who later fled from the Nazi holocaust. The thing that I got the biggest kick out of were the South African Lithuanian Jews, many of whom came from the birthplace of my father.

To the best of my knowledge, the Jewish community in South Africa is about eighty years old. The big Jewish migration from Europe came in the 1890s. That's when South Africa's famous Schlesinger family arrived. The senior Schlesinger started out as a small businessman, but through hard work and perseverance he became one of South Africa's most successful tycoons. At one time he owned most of the South African movie theaters. I was privileged to meet his son, who owned most of the Johannesburg theaters and hotels. He was a busy man, but he called Percy Tucker and asked if I could find a half hour to have tea with him in his office.

I wouldn't have missed it. In the reception rooms of his Johannesburg offices were two turbaned Indians prepared to serve tea or anything else you might want. After a short wait a secretary took me through a maze of offices to a tremendous private office, where I met the younger Schlesinger. He sat back in his chair and said, "Mickey, I've loved your work for many years. I can't go to the show tonight because unfortunately I'm leaving for London. But would you be kind enough to give me a few of your jokes?"

And while I was telling this tremendously wealthy young businessman some of my stories, other turbaned Indians were serving me goodies like a Jewish mother: little shrimps, prawns in special sauces, all sorts of cold and hot hors d'oeuvres. . . . Schlesinger kept this cordon of turbaned Indians on hand around the clock to entertain the people who came to visit him from all over the world.

For our first performance out of Johannesburg we went to Percy Tucker's hometown, Benoni, some forty miles from Johannesburg. We had dinner at his parents' home. The house was eighty years old. Percy Tucker and his European-born parents reminded me of my own family. They also spoke Yiddish as my parents had. One of my greatest fans at the Benoni concert was the little Irish Jewish fire chief, who had come to South Africa from Dublin.

After Benoni we did two shows in Durban, a fantastic city of maybe five hundred thousand, of whom 25 percent were Indians. There were maybe twenty-five hundred Jewish people. Durban, with its big Indian population, had many Mohammedan mosques. It also had an amazing curry market, a huge bazaar that must have been three blocks long, which sold every variety of curry imaginable.

A little farther on past the curry market we went into a big enclave where the natives were making jewelry. They were skilled craftsmen, whole families making marvelous jewelry and selling it to the tourists at bargain prices.

While we're talking about tourists, David Bloomberg was driving us one day from one town to another when we saw some natives alongside the road waving ostrich skins and ostrich plumes, some of the skins already made into jackets. We stopped, and Dopey and Grace got out to "shop." There beside the road they bought a couple of beautiful ostrich-skin jackets for $12 or $15 apiece—beautiful things that were worth at least $200.

At our next date, Port Elizabeth, we played in a quaint auditorium called the Feather Market, where up to a few years before, the feather merchants had auctioned the ostrich plumes and other exotic feathers once so common in South Africa.

Then we played Pretoria, the capital of South Africa. In those days the population was maybe half a million. A beautiful city of very British origin, it had the gentleness and beauty of England's Stratford-on-Avon. We played two shows in Pretoria. There's no use repeating that they loved us.

In South Africa there was only one major English-Jewish newspaper, a weekly, which told of all the doings of the Jewish communities. We saw no newspapers printed in Yiddish. If they had had any, it would have been a very small tabloid issued for the older people.

Incidentally, the newspaper reviews of our show were uniformly excellent. However, at one of our six sold-out concerts in Johannesburg, a young Jewish "intellectual" reporter from one of the Johannesburg dailies hardly enjoyed our performance. He slammed us. I think he expected a traditional Yiddish dramatic show, which is nothing we ever pretended to be.

The readers protested, "Send out another reviewer!" The paper broke precedent by sending out a second reviewer, who thought the show was wonderful. He wrote: "I didn't understand the ethnicity [!] of the show—it went a bit over my head—but the Jewish music and songs were charming and exciting. And after their regular performance, Mickey Katz and talented musician Mannie Klein, plus our own Royal Navy lads, gave us a rousing jazz concert which was beautiful to behold. They earned a standing ovation on their jazz alone. We wish them farewell, and a happy return to regale us once again with their great music of New Orleans!"

I must tell you about a special concert that we played

for the "Cape Coloureds." Coloureds are of mixed white
and black parentage, and most of them have always lived
in the Cape Town area.

The representative of the Coloureds in the South African
Parliament, since most of them lived in his district, was Abe
Bloomberg, David's father. He asked if I'd do a personal
favor for him and play a special concert for his Coloured
constituents. I said of course.

So on a free night we were driven about an hour out into
the countryside from Cape Town, where we came upon this
large colony of Coloureds.

We entered a tremendous hall, where we did an all-jazz
concert. The place was full to the rafters. I saw some faces
in the audience that were very white, others that were very
black, and many that were combinations of both.

They all went insane over our jazz music. They got up
and danced; they got up and sang. Some of them came up
on the stage and sang with us. It was one of the most memorable nights we had in South Africa.

About thirty miles down the coast from Cape Town is a
little seaside resort called Muizenberg. It's a place where
elderly Jewish people enjoy their retirement at the seashore.
Incidentally, twenty or thirty miles on south of Muizenberg
is the Cape of Good Hope—and south of that, penguins!

Anyway, this little seaside resort of Muizenberg was made
up of maybe two thousand Jewish senior citizens. They had
their Hadassah, their B'nai B'rith, and a big pavilion which
was the center for their social affairs and charitable activi-
ties. We did two sellout shows there, matinee and evening.

After the evening show a little Scots gentleman who was
representing David Bloomberg came breathlessly to our
dressing room. In a rich but hurried Scottish burr he said,
"Boys, I want you to be on your verrrry best behavior. The
rebbe [the rabbi] is coming back to see you!"

The first thing I did was caution comedian Marty Drake,
"*You* be careful! Don't open up your big mouth!"

Then we saw a man approaching who looked like Moses.

He was a beautiful tall man in rabbinical attire, and he had a flowing white beard. As he came up, I bowed and said, "*Sholem alecheim.*" ("Peace be with you" in Hebrew.)

He answered in perfect Oxford English, "Mr. Katz, I was never so thrilled in my life as by the performance you and your company have given us. It was absolutely outstanding! Mr. Klein, what a talented musician you are. And you, young man"—speaking directly to Marty Drake—"you have a lovely voice. You should be the *chazzen* [the cantor] in a synagogue."

Marty looked at me with a triumphant smirk.

We were worried about meeting the *rebbe*—he couldn't compliment us enough!

Then we were fed by the mamas of Muizenberg. "Everybody eat now!" Living there on the tip of South Africa, they were typical Yiddish mamas. It was like being back in Cleveland, with my dear mother feeding us all.

In South Africa, like England and Australia, the great percentage of the Jewish people are Orthodox or Conservative. We never did a show on Friday night. We did a show on Saturday nights after sundown, when the *Shabbes* was over.

After our last concert, in Johannesburg, we flew back to Los Angeles via Athens, Rome, and Paris. I had traveled to South Africa thinking that I would perform some shows in the jungle for the B'nai Zulu. Instead, I had a ball, playing to the nicest people I've met anywhere in the world.

Was I lucky!

13 · Grace's Faces and Meyer the Friar

IN ADDITION to being my wife, my beloved Grace has always been a talented artist. She paints pictures, she hand-paints porcelain, she makes dolls of all sorts—including life size— she makes tapestries, does needlepoint, knits, dries flower petals and makes potpourri, she hand-decorates children's furniture.

And she has been a professional success at her work. Her customers have included Cary Grant, Barbra Streisand, the late Walt Disney, Dionne Warwick, Angie Dickinson, Diana Ross, Cher. Grace has had two art galleries in Beverly Hills, in both of which she sold only her own art creations.

She has appeared with her artwork on the *Today* show with Barbara Walters and on the *Mike Douglas Show*.

Grace gets her creativity—and her beauty—from her mother. Her mother, Fanny, is now eighty-nine, and she's still beautiful. My mother-in-law had five daughters, all lovely ladies, but the others are business people. Fanny looked around at Grace's varied artwork one recent day and affectionately said, "To tell you the true, darling, you're the crap of the crop."

Even at her advanced age, my mother-in-law is still a great cook. She'll hold one of her steaming culinary triumphs aloft, and say, "Children, today I am serving something that is absolutely out-of-town."

Let me tell you an anecdote about Grandma Fanny.

Some fifteen years ago Joel was busy in both New York and Hollywood, and once a month he'd take the "red-eye special" night plane out to the Coast from New York, arriving here about five in the morning. Grace and I would drive through the predawn darkness to pick him up at the airport. Fanny observed this arrangement for a time; then she announced that the next time she'd like to go along. When we picked her up at her apartment for the drive to the airport, she was carrying an unusually large handbag. When Joel got in the car at the airport, she opened the handbag, said, "Here, eat," and handed him a thermos of her sensational barley soup.

Grace's mother was recently in a store picking out a dress. From the back of the store came a delighted cry: "Mrs. Epstein, is that you?"

Fanny went right on picking out the dress. Old acquaintances from her lengthy past she doesn't need. But after another delighted outcry of recognition, an elderly lady came around the corner of the dress rack. She said, "It *is* Mrs. Epstein!" The old lady continued, "You don't remember me? I'm Rose Levin. I used to live next door by you on Forty-sixth Street in Cleveland."

Grace's mother said, "Forty-sixth Street in Cleveland? Big deal. That was sixty years ago." The truth is that my mother-in-law, who is a very young eighty-nine, didn't want to be reminded of how long ago it was.

But the little old lady from Cleveland would not be put off. She said, "Mrs. Epstein, I want to ask you a question."

"What's that?"

"How come when we get old, we look like monkeys?"

My mother-in-law retorted in a huff, "Maybe you look like a monkey, but not me!"

And that ended that reunion.

This is the spirit and talent and love of living that Grace

inherited. Grace had her two art galleries in Beverly Hills
from 1964 to 1973. First she had a gallery in I. Magnin's department store on Wilshire Boulevard. Then she opened a
second gallery on "decorators' row" on Robertson Boulevard. The reason she wanted the second gallery was that it
was big enough for her to have a workroom in the back
where she produced her creations for both galleries. My
sister Jeanne did much of the selling, while Grace was busy
"creating" in the back room.

Grace would take a little child's footstool and hand-deco-
rate it, and somebody would come in and buy it for $50.
Her paintings sold for from $300 to $1000.

Joel would come into her "store" and look around and
protest, "Mother, your things are too expensive—you're not
Picasso." The customers happily disagreed—customers from
Red Skelton to Andy Williams to Paul Lynde, Shecky
Greene, Sally Field, and Eartha Kitt.

Grace has also painted countless pictures of children's
faces that she calls her "little people," wonderful impish
little faces looking out at you. Her young-at-heart customers
loved them.

One of the Rosenwald family of Sears, Roebuck fame
bought one of Grace's paintings. Later he invited us out to
his house in Bel-Air, to show us where he'd hung it. In one
room of his house he had a private art gallery; hung on the
walls were Chagalls, Renoirs, Van Goghs . . . and a Grace.
Rosenwald told Grace, "This is the room where I come to
meditate." He pointed to Grace's painting and added, "This
is also the room where I come to be glad that I'm alive."

Grace closed her galleries in 1973 for several reasons.
First, there was a fire at Magnin's, and when it was redeco-
rated, a whole row of shops, including Grace's gallery, was
eliminated. That started us thinking. Grace's galleries had
been a success, but they were taking an awful lot of precious
hours away from our family life. Also, Grace was tired of
working so hard; she wanted to reach out to new horizons.
So she closed the Robertson gallery, too.

While Grace was busy with her art galleries, I was busy with my shows and, among other things, the Friars Club.

The California Friars Club was founded in 1945 by George Jessel. I've been a member for twenty-five years.

The original Friars Club was, of course, founded in New York some seventy-five years ago. Today it has a beautiful clubhouse on Fifty-fifth Street off Madison Avenue.

The California Friars Club was founded by Jessel because he got tired of having to fly to New York when he felt like attending a Friars meeting. George proceeded to found a branch out here, first in a small clubhouse "on the hill" on the Sunset Strip near La Cienega. The original members included Frank Sinatra, Al Jolson, Eddie Cantor, Jack Benny, the Ritz Brothers, and Tony Martin, with Harry Cohn, Jonie Taps, and Irving Briskin of Columbia, plus Dave Siegel, Milton Krasny, and a few other important men in the movie and show-business industry—executives, producers, actors, writers. . . .

I joined in 1952. By that time the Friars had moved to Beverly Hills, to the site of the former famous Romanoff's Restaurant on Rodeo Drive. It was small, but large enough for our purposes at that time. We put on the first of our California editions of the famous "roasts" on Rodeo Drive. We'd roast Phil Silvers, Buddy Hackett, Dean Martin, Joe E. Lewis, Swifty Morgan. . . .

The Friars' roasts are hilarious affairs and, believe me, "for men only." When we roasted golfer Arnold Palmer, MC George Jessel made this observation from the dais: "What a difference a couple of letters make. Arnold Palmer has made a million dollars with his putts—my putz has cost me a million."

Johnny Carson made a wonderful crack at a recent testimonial dinner for Don Rickles: "I've known Don Rickles many years. Just this morning I saw him walking his rat."

Incidentally, the roasts have traditionally been held at the Friars Club itself; but now both the roasts and the big testimonial dinners are usually held in the International

Ballroom of the Beverly Hilton Hotel. At these latter events, with a big show and top stars, the tickets may be $75 or $175 apiece, and in one performance we may raise $100,-000 for charity.

Our first big California Friars' show—called *The Friars Frolics*—was held in 1950 at Los Angeles' Shrine Auditorium. The stars on this once-in-a-lifetime program included Al Jolson, Jack Benny, Red Skelton, George Burns. . . . In that one evening the club raised $400,000 for the Friars Charity Foundation. In the twenty-seven years since, the club has raised more than $4 million. The Friars' charity proceeds are given to needy causes without regard to race, creed, or color.

Over the years the club has gradually changed its image. The original small number of stars and movie people couldn't handle the annual expenses of running the club as others of us envisioned it. We knew that bigger things could be done, that bigger charities could be supported, if we had the money to do it. So the club started bringing in business people, from dress manufacturers to food market operators. For them the Friars made a great place to bring business guests for lunch or dinner, where they could have great food and mingle with the show people, and for the Friars the enlarged membership made for an infinitely bigger pool of funds to use in the club's charitable endeavors.

Also, it provided the funds necessary to build the Friars' present beautiful clubhouse on Santa Monica Boulevard in Beverly Hills. Here we have room for parking inside our own building, a big dining room that seats five hundred, former Friars president Milton Berle's billiard room, which he donated to the club, a fine health club with steam rooms and exercise rooms. Everything that a men's club needs—including a card room where you can play a little bridge or pinochle.

For years, starting at the small club on Rodeo, I was part of a regular bridge game consisting of George Burns, Dave Siegel, George Raft, and myself. Occasionally Chico Marx or Lou Holtz would join us, but usually we had the same players. We got a lot of laughs from the spectators and a lot of screams from the players. George Burns would make up special rules that only he understood, and he would "deadpan" insist they were right till the rest of us would give in, just to get the game going again. We played for small stakes and had a lot of laughs.

Our regular bridge quartet was so devoted to the game that we also played at each other's homes. One night we were playing at Dave Siegel's house. Dave, who was George Burns's partner, bid three no-trump. It was a disastrous bid, and they went down three, vulnerable. Burns complained, "Dave, of all the stupid bids I've ever seen, that was without doubt the most idiotic. It was the worst—"

I said, "George, this is Dave's house."

Burns deadpanned, "Sorry, Dave." And we went on with the game.

The manager of the dining room at the Friars is Jose Garcia, who has been with us a long time, and most of the dining room and kitchen employees are Mexican-Americans. Many of them speak only rudimentary English. When I was leaving the club the other afternoon, one of the waiters was unhappily pondering a lunch check. I asked him what the trouble was, and he said that Mr. Chop-iro (Shapiro) hadn't signed his lunch check. I said that he'd simply forgotten, he should sign it for him. The waiter said, "But I don't know how to spell 'Chopiro.' "

Thinking to add a little humor to the proceedings, I said, "You spell it just like you said it—C-h-o-p-i-r-o. It's a Jewish name."

Brightening, he added, "Are you Hew-ish?"

"Yes."

"You speak Jee-brew?"

I said, "*Sí*."

I have conducted the orchestra for the major functions of the Friars for twenty-five years. In recent years Jonie Taps has arranged the entertainment portion of the Friars' events, and I've led the band. Walking out there at the Beverly Hilton in a full-dress suit to conduct a thirty-piece orchestra is a glorious feeling. Unless I think of Milton Berle's line: "Mickey, in white tie and tails you look like a decoration on a bar mitzvah cake."

The most thrilling night of my life happened at the Friars. The Hollywood Musicians Union recently gave me a testimonial to commemorate my fiftieth year as a professional musician. A lot of dear friends were on the dais; they included George Jessel, Jan Murray, Rickie Layne, Jess White, Max Herman, and, for the first time in Friars dais history, many of my musicians—Mannie Klein, drummer Sammy Weiss, saxophonists Maurie Stein and Dave Harris, pianist Johnny Guarnieri, trumpeter Shorty Sherock, accordionist Johnny Largo, all of whom had played with me for the past twenty-five years. Each one did his musical specialty between speakers, and all to a standing ovation.

Incidentally, also on the dais was my son Ron, and in the front row were his sons, Randy and Todd, come to honor their grandfather and to add a few new words to their vocabularies.

A lot of nice things were said about me. But the greatest remark of the evening came before the party even started. Prior to the festivities, MC George Jessel and a few of the dais members were talking upstairs. George had been having trouble with bursitis in a shoulder, and Jan Murray asked him how he was feeling.

Jessel said, "Lousy. This bursitis is killing me."

I asked, "What are you doing for it?"

"Well, I had twenty shots of cortisone."

"Did that help?"

"Nothing."

"What else have you done?"

"Next I tried acupuncture. I was stuck with one hundred needles. Last night I dreamed I fucked a porcupine."

14 · My Son, the Computer and Everybody Give Katz de Clap

SOON AFTER MY FIRST GRANDCHILD, Randy, was born, my son Ron was working at the Bendix computer plant in Los Angeles. Ron, my college boy UCLA graduate, was earning about $110 a week to support his wife and baby. But while at Bendix, he met a young computer genius, Bob Goldman. This meeting was to change Ron's whole life.

Ronnie and Bob Goldman came up with a revolutionary system for computerized protection for check cashing. They perfected and patented their invention and called it Telecredit. Today Telecredit is in operation all over the United States. The system is as established as the Rock of Gibraltar.

But before Telecredit got off the ground, Ron told me one day that he and Bob would have to quit their jobs at Bendix and go into research for several months—research that ultimately resulted in the start of Telecredit. The boys would have to be funded during this time of no work and no dough. Bob's folks in Providence, Rhode Island, agreed to help him, and I told Ron that I would gladly see him through. Goldman's job was to perfect the computer; Ronnie's job as the business head was to find the hundreds of thousands of dollars they needed for development capital. After bitter disappointment trying to raise the money in Southern California, Ron read an ad in the *Wall Street Journal* which said, "Looking for new electronic companies that need financing." The gentleman who advertised was Morton Globus, head of a New York investment firm. Ron called Mort Globus, who came out to Los Angeles to talk to Ronnie and Bob, and to listen to their plans. Mort and Ron hit it off, and Globus agreed to raise the capital to finance the new company, Telecredit.

On a recent Sunday afternoon we went out to see Ronnie's new beach house in Malibu. And the reason I am telling you about the new house, in addition to enjoying talking about my son, is to tell you a funny incident that occurred during our inspection visit. Ron's mother-in-law, Mrs. Guttleman, was there, and so was Grace's mother. Oddly enough, they're both named Fanny. During the tour Maddie's Fanny said to Grace's Fanny, "Tell me, Fanny, how are you?"

"Very fine."

"How's your friend Bessie Glickman?"

"She's fine, but one of her sons had a terrible thing happen to him."

"What was that?"

My mother-in-law said, "If you'll excuse me, Mrs. Guttleman, I can't talk about it; to you either, Gracele, or to Maddie. This is for gentlemen only."

Grace urged her on. "Go ahead, Mama, tell us."

"Okay, you asked for it. He had cancer in the balls."

At this point I had to break in. "Good heavens, Mama, how's he getting along?"

"Just fine. They found a urology sturgeon who fixed him up, and he's now a hundred percent, thanks God."

Ronnie and I looked at each other. Then Ronnie said to his grandmother, "Grandma, how did they know that he had cancer of the balls?"

"How did they know? They took an autopsy."

My father-in-law had this same problem with his Ying-lish. I once took him to a proctologist for a rectal examination.

When I went to pick him up, he was sitting in the doctor's office with a sheet around him. As I greeted him, he suddenly started out the door. The doctor said, "Mr. Epstein, are you all right?"

He said, "I'm going to de water closet. When you was monkeying around with my ragtime, it made me had to go."

My own father always spoke of a hypo as a "highball."

Grace's Uncle Sam once came out from New Jersey. When I saw him and asked how he was getting along, he said, "I feel fine now, but when I got here, I had trouble with a toothache. The dentist said he had to pull the tooth. I said is it going to hurt me? He said I'll give you something that wouldn't hurt. He gave me something to sniff, and I sniffed and sniffed till I was conscientious."

Let me tell you just one anecdote about the days when Ronnie was getting his company started. When Ronnie was anxious for development money, a piano-player friend of mine, a tender soul, invested $3000.

And for the next year and a half he drove me insane, worrying about his money. He'd call up and say, "Hi, Mick, CHRIST ALMIGHTY, what's happening with that CRUMMY STOCK? So far it's just been a big LOSER."

I'd say, "Harold, if you're worried about the stock, I'll give you back the three thousand and take it over." At the time I had no extra $3000 to take back Harold's stock, but I was tired of his phobic anxiety.

Harold would answer, "I'm not worried, I just want to TALK about it. I just wish that somebody would REPORT to me once in a while."

"Harold, if you don't want the stock, I'll take the stock."

"I didn't SAY you should take the stock. I'd just like a little HISTORY of the PROCEEDINGS."

After several years, the stock was finally "free to sell" on the open market. But before Harold knew he could sell his, he had to take off on a long tour of Japan. The minute he got back he called his lawyer and said, "What's that Tele-credit stock doing NOW?" The lawyer told him the stock had gone up to sixty; his $3000 worth of stock was now worth $150,000.

Harold screamed, "Well, what are we waiting for? SELL IT, FOR GOD'S SAKE!"

When he actually got the money, Harold called me up and said, "Hi, Mickey; thanks to you and your wonderful son, I'm RICH!" And he sang a few bars of "Yes, I'm a Rich Man." He went on, "I'd like to take you and Grace and Ron and Maddie out to dinner. ANYPLACE! Where do you want to go?"

Well, since money was no object, I also sang four bars of "Yes, You Are a Rich Man" and decided to go to the most expensive Continental restaurant in Los Angeles. When the five of us were seated, Harold said, "Kids, the SKY'S THE LIMIT. Let's have an ORGY!"

So Grace told the waiter, "I'll have the salad vinaigrette and the lobster bisque. And I'd like some oysters to start." Maddie said she'd have the same. And I said I'd like to start with a shrimp cocktail—which was $7—and then the tour-nedos of beef, which were $28. . . . And the mushroom soup ahead of the shrimp. . . .

When the waiter got around to Harold, we'd already ordered about $200 worth of food, and Harold was looking a little shaken. He said to the waiter, "I'm not very hungry. I'll just have the salad vinaigrette, but I reserve the right to SEND IT BACK."

The waiter started bringing the food, which was, of course, out of this world. But Harold took a bite of his salad vinai-grette and said, "Heavens, this isn't salad vinaigrette, it's salad vinegar! It's no good. Kids, this is the most horrible salad I've ever had in my LIFE!"

We all said, "Now, Harold, relax." And we sang him a few more bars of "Yes, You Are a Rich Man."

We ate our way through this bacchanalian banquet. Then

the check came. Harold looked at it, turned pale, but paid it. He even managed to say, "Well, it's been a BALL, kids." Then we went out to the parking lot to get our cars. Ron and I gave our parking checks to the attendant, but Harold started walking away. I said, "Harold, didn't you drive?"

He said, "Yes, but I parked MINE a couple of blocks away on the STREET. Basically, I'm CHEAP."

And he went walking off into the night, after spending $225; then he began singing in a soft pianissimo, "So what, I'm still a rich man!"

Neither of my sons achieved success the easy way. Like Joel, Ron worked hard. Several years ago, with Telecredit firmly established, he turned the active management of the company over to a brilliant executive who had been associated with him in the early years. Lee Ault III, Ivy League but with terrific business acumen. Lee Ault has done a sensational job. Ron now spends most of his own time finding unsuccessful companies and turning them into successful companies.

Ron and Maddie have two fine sons—Randy, nineteen, now in his third year at Yale, and young Todd, fifteen. Both the boys love tennis, and they're both fine players. For several years they've had a UCLA tennis tournament star living with them—Ferdie Taygan—who they're sure is going to be another Jimmy Connors. In addition to the family's sports interest, Maddie is a gourmet cook, and she is very active in all charitable endeavors.

Our sons and their families are very close. Joel and Jo recently moved into a new apartment in New York, where they have a guest room especially for Randy when he comes in on weekends from New Haven. Joel calls his own family "The four Js"—Joel, Jo, Jennifer, and Jim. Jennifer is a delightful and beautiful girl of seventeen who loves the theater and who in my opinion may well become a part of it. Jim is a towheaded youngster just entering his teens. Recently, when he began studying for his bar mitzvah, he called me from New York and asked me what his Hebrew

name was, so that he could inform his bar mitzvah teacher.
I said, "Your name in Hebrew is Yehoshuah [Joshua]." He
said, "Yehoshuwa? What am I—Japanese?"

Lately, I'm in a brand-new kind of show business—the
Florida "condominium circuit," which for entertainers has
become a whole new source of income.

That reminds me of a story. Two ladies met in Miami
Beach, and one said, "Wish me a happy birthday!"

"Happy birthday, darling. Did you get presents?"

"You should know what I got from my husband. Next
week we're going on a trip around the world."

"Dot's nice. I just had a birthday also."

"What did your husband give you?"

"He gave me a condominium."

"Is that so? We're still using the pill."

Then there were the two elderly gentlemen who bought
a Florida condominium together. One walked in one day
and heard the water running noisily in the bathtub. He
looked in the bathroom and to his amazement saw his condominium mate sitting in the bathtub, his *yarmulke* on his
head, his *talis* (prayer shawl) around his shoulders, silently
reading his prayer book, and rocking reverently back and
forth.

His friend said, "Are you crazy! Sitting in a bathtub with
a *yarmulke* and a *talis, davening* [praying]? I'm going to
send for the guy with the white jacket."

His roommate looked up soulfully and said, "The doctor
said I have to take a hot bath every day religiously."

Senior citizens by the thousands have flocked to the condominiums in Florida to retire because that's where they
can enjoy life on what they can afford. In many areas they
can buy a beautiful condominium for $18,000 or $20,000—
a third down and maybe $250 a month, to cover the mortgage
payment, the maintenance, and the taxes. On an income of
maybe $750 a month these people live just fine. They have
every necessary convenience, including auditoriums right

in their condominium complexes where they can now see some of the top stars of show business for $1.50 or $2 a ticket.

It's this circuit of big condominiums encompassing five hundred to one thousand apartments each that makes up the Florida condominium circuit. One of the agencies booking these Florida attractions is Jerry Grant, and his co-bookers are former child movie star Bobby Breen and Bobby's wife, Audrey. Another power in the condo booking is Arie Kaduri, who came to Miami Beach from Israel.

This was my schedule on the condo circuit: I would do two shows a night, one each at two different condominiums. The first show would be at seven-thirty. There would be two acts in front of me—usually another comedian and a vocalist.

The opening comedian would do twenty minutes; then the vocalist would do thirty minutes. Then I would come on for forty or forty-five minutes and close the show. The musical background was three pieces—piano, drums, and trumpet.

While I was on, the first two acts had already left and were about to start the show at the second condominium, which started at nine. When I finished at the first place, I was chauffeured over to the second condo, where I went on at ten.

In my forty-five or fifty minutes I told jokes, sang a few songs, and played some happy Jewish folk music on my clarinet with the band. I'd also play some jazz—whatever was necessary to leave these wonderful people happy.

For me, of course, playing the Florida condominium circuit is like old home week. So many of my old fans are there, and so many of my old friends.

The audiences are not to be believed. Every night at the end of my act they literally stand up and cheer. One night at the end of my performance an old gentleman got so excited that he jumped up and cried, "Everybody give Katz de clap!"

I said, "At this time of my life, I don't need it." It brought a howl, and from then on the joke followed me all over the circuit.

After a performance one night at a condominium in Fort Lauderdale a little lady came up to me and asked, "Is your son Joel Grey?"

I said, "Yes."

She continued, "What was his name before it was Grey?"

I said, "Katz."

She answered, "You know, I thought so."

My dear friend comedian Jan Murray was playing the condo circuit, and one night he was doing his hilarious routine spoofing TV commercials—how the toothpaste and the aspirin and the detergents jazz up their commercials to make you buy the product at high prices.

Just then a little old lady in the audience popped up. "But Mr. Murray," she said, "aren't you happy they named the cat Morris?"

One night at the ten o'clock show at the evening's second condominium, I was waiting in the wings offstage to go on, when a small elderly gentleman walked up to me and excitedly said, "I know you for thirty years. What's your name?"

Many of my retired Florida fans forget that I started in show business quite young. One night a gentleman cornered me after my show. In a hushed voice he said, "I'm from Cleveland, and I know you for fifty years."

I said, "That's nice," and tried to move on.

He grabbed me and whispered in my ear, "You see that guy standing behind me? I made a dollar bet with him. He says you're seventy-six; I say you're seventy-eight."

I answered with a smile. "You're both wrong, I'm sixty-eight."

He retorted, "Katz, you can give 'em dot crap in California, but I know you're seventy-eight."

Believe me, I'm only sixty-eight. I still love to play my clarinet. I still love to make people laugh. I can still fit into my size 37 tuxedo, and I'm still available for weddings, bar mitzvahs, and brisses.

Yours, lox, stock, and bagel,

MICKEY KATZ